Acoustics
IN ARCHITECTURAL
DESIGN

Acoustics
IN ARCHITECTURAL
DESIGN

THE CROWOOD PRESS

First published in 2021 by
The Crowood Press Ltd
Ramsbury, Marlborough
Wiltshire SN8 2HR

enquiries@crowood.com
www.crowood.com

British Library Cataloguing-in-Publication Data
A catalogue record for this book is available from the British Library.

ISBN 978 1 78500 878 8

Cover design by Sergey Tsvetkov

Typeset by Simon and Sons
Printed and bound in India by Replika Press Pvt. Ltd.

Contents

Introduction ～ 6

Chapter One　　Fundamentals of Acoustics ～ 8

Chapter Two　　Opera Houses and Concert Halls (Pre-Twentieth Century) ～ 29

Chapter Three　Opera Houses and Concert Halls
　　　　　　　　(Twentieth to Twenty-First Centuries) ～ 46

Chapter Four　　The Acoustics of Theatres ～ 81

Chapter Five　　The Acoustics of Schools ～ 96

Chapter Six　　Music Schools and Recital Halls ～ 110

Chapter Seven　Other Building Types ～ 137

Conclusion: Future Possibilities ～ 152

Glossary of Acoustical Terms ～ 154

Acknowledgements ～ 155

References ～ 156

Index ～ 158

THE FRENCH ARCHITECT, LE CORBUSIER, regarded as one of the fathers of modernism, is quoted as saying that 'Architects have a feeling for space'. He could have said the same thing about acousticians, although he would have been talking about quite a different perception of space. Architects sense space by visual cues, whilst acousticians sense space by aural cues. This difference was highlighted rather starkly in a lecture course to architecture and engineering students by Robert E. Apfel at Yale University, which was entitled 'Deaf architects and blind acousticians'.

This sensing of space using aural cues goes right back to the Stone Age, where people explored tunnels and caves in the dark and made noises to find spaces that were more resonant or reverberant. When they located such spaces they painted pictures on the walls, which are still evident today, and it is suggested that some of these caves may have been used for rituals or initiation ceremonies.

The beginnings of the understanding of acoustics can be traced back to the sixth century BC, when it is thought that the Greek mathematician Pythagoras had worked out that sound is a vibration transmitted from a source to the ear. In fact the word 'acoustics' comes from the Greek *akoúō*, which means 'to hear'.

The Greeks went on to build some spectacular theatres, the most famous of which is the theatre at Epidaurus, built in the fourth century BC. It is still in existence today, and is reputed to have excellent acoustics – it will be discussed in more detail in Chapters 1 and 2.

The Romans followed on from the Greeks in building theatres, and in the first century BC the Roman architect Vitruvius documented the principles of theatre design is his *Ten Books of Architecture*. This is a very important document, as it not only tells us the Roman approach to building theatres, including ideas on acoustics, but it influenced the resurgence of theatre construction in the Renaissance period.

Leading Renaissance architects such as Palladio were influenced by Vitruvius' writings: this is evident in the plan shapes they designed, which are based on the amphitheatre model (Palladio's theatre, the Teatro Olimpico, is discussed in Chapter 4). These amphitheatre-type designs later developed into the horseshoe plan shape typical of opera houses in the eighteenth and nineteenth centuries, a tradition that continues into the twenty-first century.

In terms of acoustics, little progress was made in developing the science of architectural acoustics before the twentieth century. The Italian architect, Niccolini, designer of the Teatro San Carlo in Naples (1817), wrote 'Until the present day, the nature of sound propagation is considered by many as an unknown mystery'. Even in the late nineteenth century the subject was still largely considered a mystery. The eminent Viennese architect Adolf Loos published an essay in 1912 entitled *Das Mysterium der Akustik*, in which he said that concert halls become acoustically excellent when fine music played in them is gradually absorbed by the walls. In the mortar, he said, live the sounds of the great composers. But brass instruments, he warned, have a bad effect, and military music can ruin the acoustics within a week.

The breakthrough in architectural acoustics came at the turn of the twentieth century when Harvard professor, Wallace Clement Sabine, developed his theory of reverberation and effectively became the father of modern architectural acoustics. Sabine proposed the concept of 'reverberation time' (RT), which is approximately the time it takes in seconds for a loud sound in a room, when stopped, to decay to inaudibility. He showed that reverberation time is linked to intelligibility of speech – short RTs give good intelligibility, whilst long RTs make speech less clear.

He showed that reverberation time is directly proportional to the volume of a room, and inversely proportional to the total acoustic absorption. Sabine's equation, which is seductively simple, has profoundly influenced room acoustics throughout the twentieth century, and continues to do so in the twenty-first. Further details of the equation and examples of its use are described in Chapter 1.

Following Chapter 1, which provides an introduction to the fundamentals of acoustics, the book proceeds to look at the relationship between acoustics and the architectural design of various building types. Starting with the design of auditoria, which is perhaps where acoustics is particularly prominent, a description is given of the evolution of auditoria for opera, music and theatre. This is followed by the acoustic design of schools, which, relatively recently, has been influenced by regulation in England and Wales in a highly beneficial way. Other building types then follow, such as worship spaces, law courts, museums, transportation buildings, and open plan offices.

This book should be of interest to architecture students and their qualified colleagues, musicians, theatre consultants, acousticians, building engineers, and those who procure and manage buildings where acoustics is of fundamental importance.

Chapter One

Fundamentals of Acoustics

Definitions of Sound

An early definition of sound comes from the Roman architect, Vitruvius, who lived in the first century BC. In his writings on architecture, contained in *The Ten Books of Architecture* (translated by M.H. Morgan, 1960), he wrote the following description about the nature of sound produced by the voice:

> Voice is a flowing breath of air, perceptible to the hearing by contact. It moves in an endless number of circular rounds, like the innumerably increasing circular waves which appear when a stone is thrown into smooth water ... but while in the case of water the circles move horizontally on the plane surface, the voice not only proceeds horizontally, but also vertically in regular stages.

This is a useful definition as it enables us to picture sound waves travelling outwards from a source as a series of expanding concentric spheres (Fig. 1.1). As the distance from the source increases, the amplitude of the waves will gradually diminish.

Another, more modern definition, is that sound is a disturbance that propagates in an elastic medium, such as air, at a speed that is characteristic of that medium. This establishes that the speed of sound is constant in air. In fact it is 343m/sec at 20°C. The variation with temperature is very small, so this is not a concern in architectural acoustics. The term 'disturbance' in the above definition usually means there is a vibrating object, such as a vibrating tuning fork or a loudspeaker diaphragm, which is compressing and expanding the air adjacent to it and hence generating sound waves.

A third definition is that sound is a sensation perceptible to the human and animal hearing systems. The nature of the human hearing system will be discussed a little later.

Fig. 1.1 Circular waves when a stone is thrown into still water. (Photo: Alamy)

Wavelength and Frequency

Fig. 1.2 illustrates the sound wave of a pure tone such as a steady whistle. The vertical axis represents pressure, and the waveform shows variations in air pressure relative to atmospheric pressure. These variations are very much smaller than the atmospheric pressure itself. The horizontal axis represents time or distance from the source. The first part of the wave shows a steady increase in air pressure from zero to a maximum, followed by a steady decrease back down to zero. This part of the wave is called a compression. The second part of the wave shows a decrease below atmospheric pressure down to a minimum, which then rises back to zero. This is called a rarefaction. The cycle then repeats itself. So a sound wave basically consists of a series of compressions and rarefactions.

If the number of cycles of the sound wave occurs more quickly in a given time period than in Fig. 1.2, the pitch of the sound increases. Conversely, if fewer cycles occur, the pitch of the sound decreases. This is illustrated in Fig. 1.3.

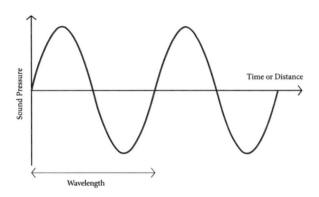

Fig. 1.2 Sound wave of a pure tone.

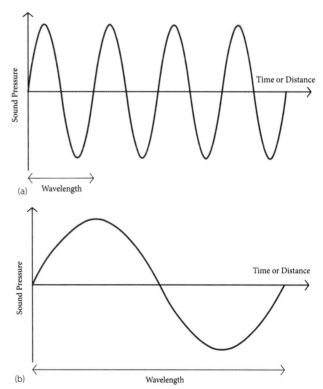

Fig. 1.3 High frequency sound wave (a, above) relative to low frequency sound wave (b, below).

(a)

(b)

The number of cycles occurring in one second is referred to as the frequency of the sound which has the unit hertz (Hz). So, for example, the middle C note on a piano generates 262 cycles per second, or 262Hz.

The other key parameter of the wave in Figs 1.2 and 1.3 is the distance between repetitions – this is referred to as the wavelength, and is measured in metres. Sound waves obey the same rules as other wave motions, where the fundamental relationship is:

$$Speed = frequency \times wavelength$$

As the speed of sound in air is constant, then the frequency is inversely proportional to the wavelength; this means that as the frequency increases, the wavelength decreases, and vice versa.

It is useful to know the range of wavelengths occurring in architectural acoustics. The wavelength of the middle C note on the piano is 1.3m. The lowest note on a bass guitar or double bass, which has a frequency of 40Hz, has a wavelength of 8.6m. By contrast, the highest note on a piccolo, which has a frequency of 4,000Hz, has a wavelength of 0.086m, or 8.7cm.

The relationship between the wavelengths of sound and the dimensions of rooms, buildings and other constructions in the built environment is very relevant.

For example, consider a tall fence, say 2.5m (8ft) high, alongside a motorway: the road traffic noise will be quieter on the far side of the fence but remains audible because the sound waves bend around the top of the fence; this bending effect is called 'diffraction'. As well as being quieter on the far side, the quality

of the sound will be different: it will be more of a 'rumble' without the 'hiss'. This is because long waves (low frequencies) bend easily around obstacles, whereas short wavelengths (high frequencies) bend very little and create a shadow zone. This is illustrated in Fig. 1.4.

In general, long waves bend around most obstacles and continue along their path, whereas short wavelengths create a shadow zone because they bend very little.

Now consider sound in a room: if the wavelength of the sound is the same as one of the room dimensions, say the distance between two parallel opposite walls, then the sound energy in the wave will become trapped between the two surfaces and will oscillate backwards and forwards forming a resonance – rather like an organ pipe. These resonances are called standing waves, and the sound energy in them can persist longer than other sound reflections in the room. The effect is most obvious in small rooms, and is one of the reasons why singing in a bathroom can sound very effective when these strong resonances are hit upon!

Standing waves also occur when two waves, three waves, four waves and so on fit into a room dimension. They also occur in each of the three main room dimensions, and even in the diagonals of the room. So for a room of any given size, there will be a number of frequencies where standing waves will be formed, and at these frequencies the sound will be accentuated and will tend to persist longer than other sounds.

The number of standing waves, or normal modes as they are sometimes called, in a typical room will

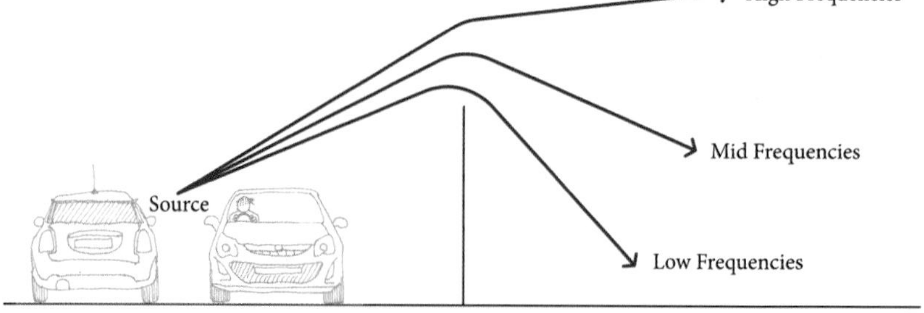

Fig. 1.4 The effect of a barrier at different sound frequencies.

High Frequencies

Mid Frequencies

Source

Low Frequencies

be very large, and when the room dimensions are at least as large as the wavelength of the lowest frequency of sound, say 10m (33ft), then the modes are closely spaced in frequency and no particular sound will become prominent. However, in small rooms, normal modes are spaced more widely at low frequencies, and then individual frequencies can be strongly accentuated. This is particularly the case if two or more of the room dimensions are the same, or related by simple ratios such as 2:1.

This can be a particular problem in rooms where it is important to preserve the true quality of the sound, such as music practice rooms and recording studios. In the design of such rooms it is important to avoid the same room dimensions or simple ratios of dimensions so as to avoid strong standing waves, which could distort, or colour, the sound.

Measuring Levels of Sound: The Decibel

The range of sound pressures to which the ear is sensitive is very large, over one million to one. If these sound pressures were to be measured in standard units of pressure – namely, pascals – then the quietest sound that can be heard would be around 0.00002 pascals (Pa) or 20 micropascals (µPa) – this is generally considered to be the threshold of hearing. At the other end of the scale, one of the loudest sounds that can be heard has a sound pressure of 20Pa – this is around the threshold of pain when 'tingling' starts to occur in the ears. So using pascals to measure sound pressure would lead to a very inconvenient set of numbers. It would be much easier to have a scale such as the centigrade scale for temperature, which has a hundred divisions.

As a first step, it is useful to express any particular sound pressure as a ratio with reference to the quietest sound we can hear. This reference is taken to be 20µPa at 1000Hz, and forms an international standard. However, using this ratio still leaves us with a range of around a million numbers.

Instead of using unit increases in sound pressure, if we considered the number of factors of 10 increase, this would considerably reduce our range of numbers. This calculation is done simply by taking the logarithm of the number to base 10.

This concept correlates reasonably well with the way our ears perceive different levels of sound pressure. They do not respond equally to equal changes in sound pressure, but rather they respond to a given sound pressure by relating it to the sound pressure they were already hearing. This psychoacoustic effect is true not just for sound but for other senses, and is referred to as the Weber-Fechner law (Yost 2000). An example can be shown visually by viewing the two pairs of boxes in Fig. 1.5.

In the left-hand pair, the lower box has ten more dots, and it is clear that a substantial increase in dots has occurred. In the right-hand pair, the lower box also has ten more dots but this is not clearly evident. The lower right-hand box would require one hundred additional dots to be perceived as the same increase. This is, in fact, a logarithmic relationship, and one that should be followed in developing a scale for perceived levels of sound pressure.

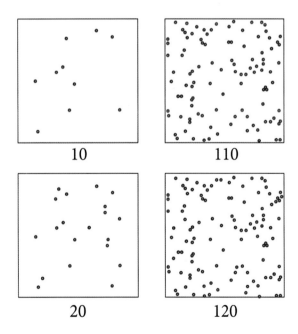

Fig. 1.5 Visual depiction of Weber-Fechner Law.

A logarithmic unit was already available for measuring the power loss along telephone lines and was named the bel, after Alexander Graham Bell, the inventor of the telephone. However, this unit dealt with power rather than voltage (voltage in electrical terms can be considered equivalent to pressure in acoustical terms), and to adopt this unit the values of sound pressure would have to be squared, as power is proportional to pressure squared. To evaluate the sound pressure in bels, the relationship is as follows:

$$\text{Logarithm to base 10 } \frac{(\text{sound pressure})^2}{(\text{reference pressure})^2}$$

This provides a range of numbers according to the following calculation:

$$\text{Logarithm to base 10 } \frac{(20 \text{ pascals})^2}{(20 \times 10^{-6} \text{ pascals})^2} = 12$$

This now turns out to be a very small range of numbers to cover the very loudest sounds to the very quietest. Therefore it was decided to multiply the bel by a factor of 10 and call it the decibel (abbreviated dB). This now provides a range of numbers from 0 to 120, which has proved highly suitable for measuring the sound pressures in the human hearing range.

The key equation is:

$$\text{Sound Pressure Level} = 10 \log_{10} \frac{(\text{pressure})^2}{(\text{reference pressure})^2}$$

$$= 20 \log_{10} \frac{(\text{pressure})}{(\text{reference pressure})}$$

Note that whenever the term 'level' is included after 'sound pressure' – that is, 'sound pressure level' – this means that the decibel scale is being used.

Examples of using the decibel scale are as follows. If the sound pressure is doubled, this results in an increase of sound pressure level of 6dB. This is a clearly audible change. By contrast, if the sound pressure is increased by around 12 per cent, the increase in sound pressure level is 1dB: this change is just about audible to the attentive listener. An increase in sound pressure of 40 per cent gives an increase in

decibels of 3dB; this is considered to be an audible change in most circumstances. An approximately three-fold increase in sound pressure equates to around a 10dB increase; this is considered subjectively as a doubling of loudness.

In subjective terms, the above examples are approximations, but are useful when making general observations. It is necessary to be aware of the type of signal being listened to, in particular its spectral content, as the ear has different sensitivities to different frequencies of sound.

The Response of the Ear

It has already been said that at 1000Hz, the ear can just perceive a sound pressure of 20μPa (equivalent to 0dB). The ear is slightly more sensitive in the frequency range 3000Hz to 5000Hz, by about 4dB. However, as the frequency lowers, the ear gets progressively less sensitive, so that at 125Hz the ear is around 20dB less sensitive. So the ear has a very uneven response to different frequencies of sound: in essence it is less sensitive to low frequency sound compared with mid and high frequency sound; it is also a bit less sensitive to very high frequency sounds. However, as the loudness of sound increases, this unevenness in sensitivity becomes less pronounced, so that with very loud sounds, such as those that might be experienced at a rock concert, the sensitivity to different frequencies becomes almost the same.

These different responses of the ear can be represented on a graph as a series of curves, each curve representing the sensitivity of the ear to different frequencies, and also at different levels from the threshold of hearing to the threshold of pain. These are called equal loudness curves and are shown in Fig. 1.6. The loudness along each curve remains the same, although the sound pressure level varies because of the variation in the sensitivity of the ear to different frequencies; each curve is referred to as a number of phons where the value of the phon corresponds to the sound pressure level at 1kHz.

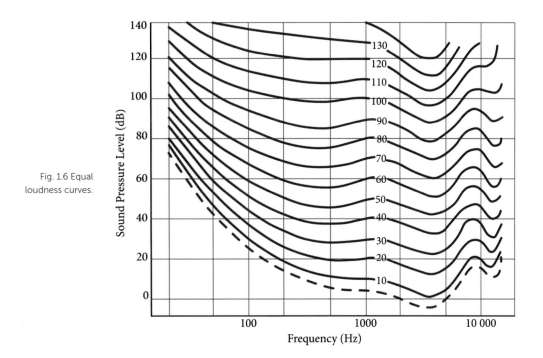

Fig. 1.6 Equal loudness curves.

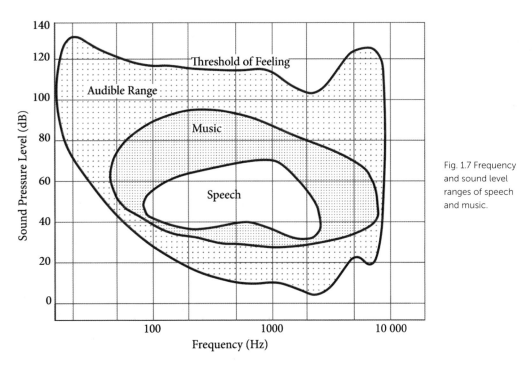

Fig. 1.7 Frequency and sound level ranges of speech and music.

It is interesting to compare the range of human hearing with the range of speech and music; this is shown in Fig. 1.7. Note that music has a significantly greater range than speech.

When measurements of sound are made, it is useful to have a single number that correlates with the way the ear perceives the loudness of a sound. A measurement microphone will usually have a constant response to the range of frequencies audible by the human ear, and so will not replicate the insensitivity of the ear to low frequencies and very high frequencies. To do this, an electronic filter is introduced after the microphone, which mimics the response of the human ear. This filter cannot mimic the different responses at different sound levels, and so a standard filter curve has been adopted based on the equal loudness curve at a level of 40 phons.

The response of this filter is shown in Fig. 1.8, where it can be seen that the filter reduces the signal gradually as the frequency decreases, in the same way that the ear does. The frequency weighting of this filter is termed an A-weighting, and sound levels measured with this filter are denoted as dBA.

It is useful to consider everyday sounds in terms of their sound levels in dBA. These are set out in Fig. 1.9. Note that it is very rare to experience sound levels below 20dBA as this requires ambient noise such as road traffic and birdsong to be excluded from a space; broadcast studios and concert halls can have such low sound levels.

When considering acoustics in engineering terms – where, for example, there might be a need to reduce the noise of a large ventilation fan – a single figure number in dBA is not sufficient to implement noise-control measures, such as specifying a silencer. It is necessary to consider the noise of the fan at different frequencies, and to do this, the frequency spectrum is divided into bands that cover the audible spectrum.

The convention that has been adopted for these frequency bands is that they are divided into octaves where the uppermost frequency in each band is twice the lower frequency. (These octaves are the same octaves as used in music.) Furthermore, the positioning of the octave bands in the

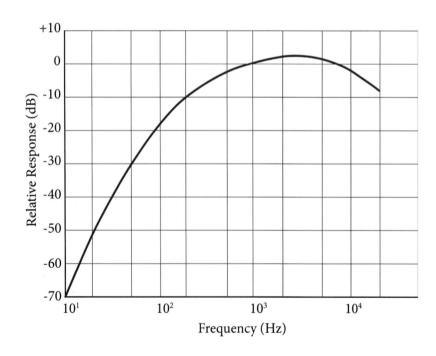

Fig. 1.8
A-weighting
curve.

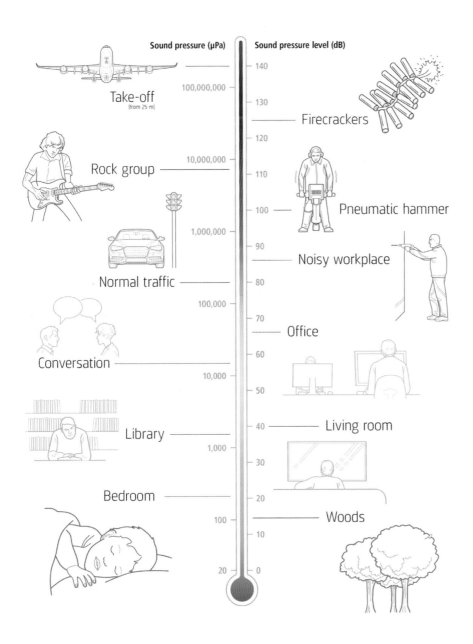

frequency spectrum follows an international standard where each band is referred to by its centre frequency. So around the centre of the spectrum there is the 1000Hz band, and below this there is the 500Hz band, 250Hz band, 125Hz band and so on. Above 1000Hz, there are the 2000Hz, 4000Hz bands and so on. These octave bands are shown in Fig. 1.10.

For more detailed analysis, each octave band can be split into three third-octave bands, and for even finer analysis, narrower bands can be used, which is termed narrow-band analysis.

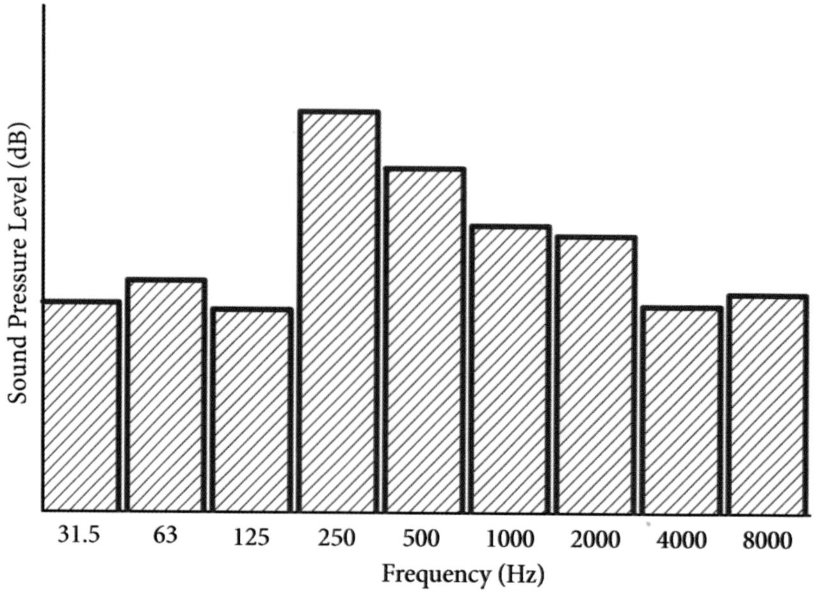

Fig. 1.10 Sound spectrum divided into octave bands.

Elements of Room Acoustics

In introducing room acoustics, it is useful to first consider sound outdoors as might have been experienced in a traditional Greek theatre such as the one at Epidaurus (Fig. 1.11). This theatre is dealt with in more detail in Chapter 2, but serves here as a useful introduction.

The speech sounds from an actor on the stage of the Greek theatre will reach a listener first by the direct path, as shown in the section in Fig. 1.12; this is called the direct sound. Very shortly afterwards, the listener will receive a repetition of the direct sound via a reflected path where the reflection is from the stage: this is called an early reflection.

If we wanted to record the acoustic characteristics between the speaker and listener in the theatre, we could make an impulsive sound at the location of the speaker, such as a hand-clap or gun shot, and measure the response at the location of the listener. This response would look like the plot adjacent to the section where we can see the direct pulse arriving

at the listener, followed by a second pulse that is smaller in amplitude because it has travelled further and also lost some energy on reflection. This type of plot is very important in room acoustics, and is called an impulse response – it shows the sequence of reflections following the direct sound and their time delays.

Considering now the sound between speaker and listener in a more conventional theatre with a roof, there are now not one, but a multitude of reflections following the direct sound. These reflections are generated by the ceiling, the walls, and all the other surfaces and objects in the theatre, as shown in Fig. 1.13. If the impulse response is measured between speaker and listener in this space, it is much more complex than in Greek theatre, as shown in the associated plot.

This impulse response can usefully be divided into two parts: the first part includes the direct sound and early reflections, and these early reflections are generally considered to arrive within a tenth of a second of the direct sound. In the second part,

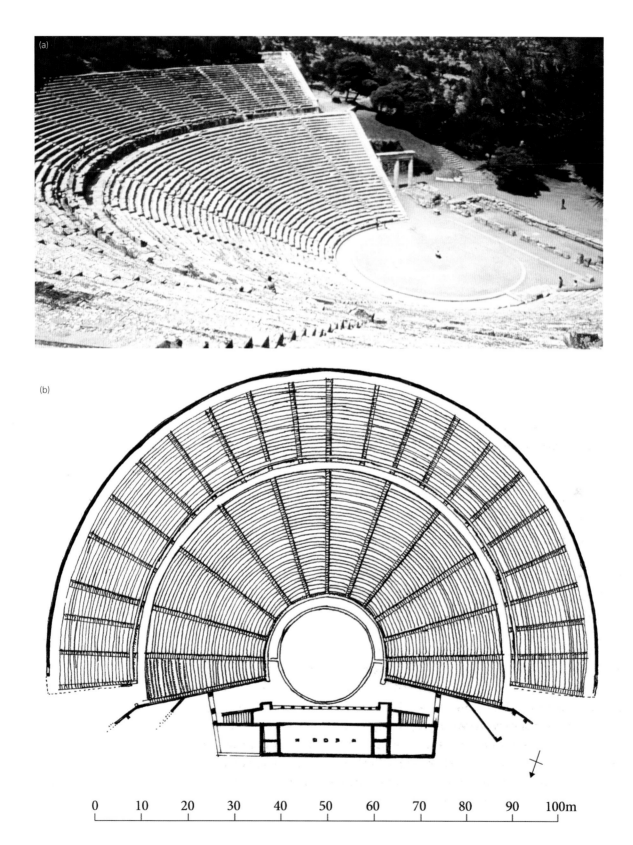

Fig. 1.11 Epidaurus amphitheatre (a) and plan (b).

(a)

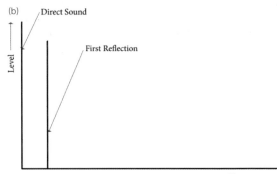

(b)

Direct Sound

First Reflection

Level

Time

Fig. 1.12 Direct sound and reflection at Epidaurus (a), and the resulting impulse response (b).

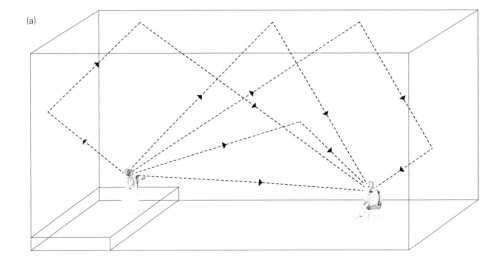

(a)

Fig. 1.13 Sound reflections in a room (a) and the resulting impulse response (b).

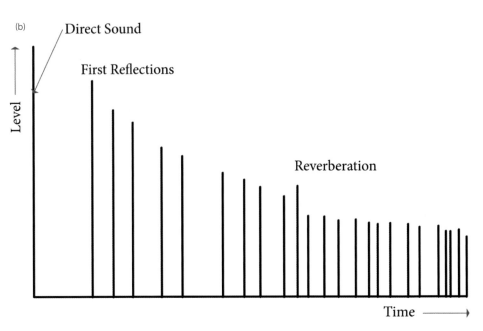

(b)

Direct Sound

First Reflections

Reverberation

Level

Time

the reflections become much denser, and gradually diminish in amplitude; these reflections are called late reflections or reverberation.

In listening to sound in a room, it is clear that each individual reflection is not heard, otherwise there would be a cacophony of sound. The ear and brain integrate the early reflections with the direct sound, and this adds to the loudness of the direct sound and enhances overall clarity. The later reflections are heard as a reverberant decaying tail, referred to as 'reverberation'. The balance between early and late reflections is fundamental to the quality of the sound that we hear.

Reverberation

The length of the reverberation in seconds depends on the type of room being considered: in a cathedral the reverberation can be very long, up to 10 seconds or more, whereas in a typical domestic living room it will be around 0.5 seconds.

When listening to speech or music in a room, each individual syllable or note will have a reverberant tail, and if the reverberation is long, as in a cathedral, this tail will run into the next syllable or note and will mask it to some extent, making speech difficult to understand and music indistinct. This is depicted in the lower diagram in Fig. 1.14.

By contrast, if the reverberation time is short, each syllable or note will stand out more clearly, and the tail will impinge less on its neighbour; this is shown in the upper diagram – in this case speech will be clear and music distinct.

However, there are different requirements for speech and music: speech requires a shorter duration of reverberation than music to provide good intelligibility, whereas in music the notes need to flow into each other to a certain extent. So there is an optimum value for the duration of reverberation for speech, which is around 1 second and an optimum one for music, which is typically around 2 seconds (depending on the style of music).

The duration of reverberation is called the 'reverberation time', and the theory of reverberation was developed at the turn of the twentieth century by a Harvard professor, Wallace Clement Sabine.

Sabine's work on reverberation was initiated at Harvard University because a new lecture theatre,

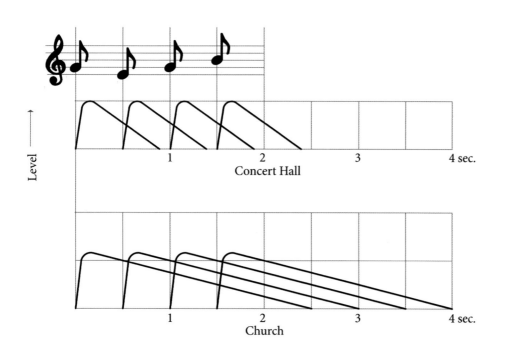

Fig. 1.14 Comparison of sound decays in a concert hall and a church.

housed in the Fogg Art Museum, had quickly gained a reputation for very poor acoustics for speech. The lecture theatre, opened in 1895, was designed according to the classical Greek form, and is shown in plan and section in Fig. 1.15. The President of the University invited Sabine, an assistant physics professor at the time, to investigate the problem and to come up with a solution. This led to a fundamental breakthrough in architectural acoustics, and gave birth to the modern science of acoustics.

Sabine developed a simple method of measuring the persistence of sound based on using an organ pipe and a stop watch. He found that the reverberation time in the empty lecture theatre was 5.5 seconds. Sabine explained the problem of this long reverberation time as follows:

During this time [reverberation time] even a very deliberate speaker would have uttered the twelve or fifteen succeeding syllables. Thus the successive enunciations blended into a loud sound, through which and above which it was

necessary to hear and distinguish the orderly progression of the speech. Across the room this could not be done; even near the speaker it could be done only with an effort wearisome in the extreme if long maintained. (Sabine 1922)

Sabine then proceeded to install lines of cushions into the lecture theatre, and measured the reduction in reverberation time at each stage. He found that by installing cushions on all the seats, the aisles, the platform and the rear wall, the reverberation time was reduced to 0.75 seconds. He also found that the graph plotting the reverberation time against the amount of acoustic absorption was a rectangular hyperbola. He thus showed that reverberation time is inversely proportional to the amount of absorption.

Sabine repeated his experiment in rooms of different sizes and further found that the reverberation time is proportional to room volume. He thus came up with the most fundamental relationship in architectural acoustics, which relates reverberation time

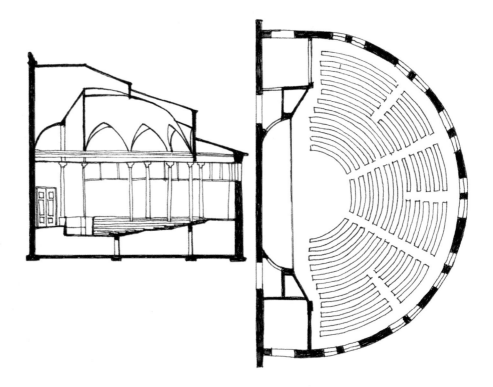

Fig. 1.15 Plan and section of the lecture theatre at the Fogg Art Museum.

to room volume and total acoustic absorption. He expressed this finding in his paper on the subject rather modestly, as follows:

> We have thus at hand a ready method of calculating the reverberation for any room, its volume and the materials of which it is composed being known.

The relationship is quite rightly known universally as Sabine's equation, and the underlying theory as Sabine's theory. The equation in metric units can be written as follows:

Reverberation Time, (T) (seconds)

$$= \frac{0.16 \times \text{Volume (V)}}{\text{Total acoustic absorption (A)}}$$

$$T = \frac{0.16V}{A}$$

Sabine's equation is fundamental to room acoustics, and remains the most important method for calculating the reverberation time in a room. Calculating the volume of a room is usually straightforward, although it can be tricky with complex geometries such as sometimes occur in theatres. The total acoustic absorption is calculated by taking the area of each surface (S) in the room and multiplying it by its absorbing power (the absorption coefficient of the material (α) – see next section for definition) giving S α. Then the absorptions of all the surfaces are added together, giving the total absorption, A:

$$A = (S_1 \, \alpha_1 + S_2 \, \alpha_2 + S_3 \, \alpha_3 + S_4 \, \alpha_4 \ldots \ldots)$$

As an example, a simple calculation can be carried out of the reverberation time of a concert hall. It is assumed that the concert hall is shaped like a large shoebox with length, width and height dimensions of $36 \times 20 \times 16$m ($98 \times 66 \times 52$ft). It is further assumed that the walls and ceiling are of plastered masonry, and that the whole floor is covered by audience and orchestra. The volume of the concert hall is therefore 11,520m^3 (15,068yd^3) and the surface area of the

walls and ceiling is 2,512m^2 (3,004yd^2). Assuming a sound absorption coefficient of 0.1 for the walls and ceiling (this means 10 per cent of the incident sound is absorbed), their total absorption is 251.2m^2. The audience is much more absorbing and will have an absorption coefficient of around 0.9, which puts the absorption of the audience at 648m^2. The total acoustic absorption in the hall is therefore 899m^2. The reverberation time can now be calculated by Sabine's equation where

$$T = \frac{0.16 \times 11520}{899} = 2 \text{ seconds}$$

This is a typical value for a concert hall for orchestral music.

Reverberation time is measured following the international standard procedure: namely, to determine the time taken in seconds for a sound, when stopped, to decay by 60dB.

Traditionally, reverberation time is measured by making a loud impulsive sound, such as a gun shot, and recording the decay of the sound level. The slope of the decay is measured using a calibrated protractor, giving an answer in seconds. An alternative method involves radiating a noise signal from a loudspeaker, which is switched off and the resulting decay recorded. Fig. 1.16 illustrates the type of decay curve that is produced, which is not totally smooth but has small fluctuations. In practice, it is not usually possible to measure the full decay over 60dB due to limitations of instrumentation, and so the measurement is taken from a point 5dB below the peak level to 35dB below (a 30dB range) – the time period measured is then multiplied by two to represent the full 60dB range.

Present-day equipment measures the reverberation time digitally and gives a numerical readout, although the decay curves can still be viewed to see if there are any irregularities. One such irregularity could be a prominent peak along the decay, which would indicate a strong echo – this could be problematic in a theatre or concert hall.

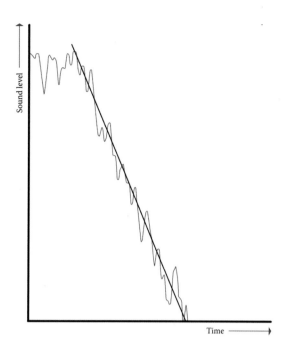

Fig. 1.16 A typical decay curve.

Although reverberation time remains the most important room acoustics parameter, it is rare to hear the full 60dB reverberant decay in a room – though sometimes this may be possible when, for example, the orchestra plays a loud chord at the end of a symphony. It is more usual to hear the partial decay between individual notes as the music is being played, during so-called 'running music'. Based on this concept, a measure called the 'early decay time' (EDT) was developed, which evaluates the time taken for the first 10dB of decay. This value is then multiplied by six so that a direct comparison can be made with reverberation time.

In a space that is highly diffuse – that is, when the sound energy is travelling equally in all directions – the early decay time and the reverberation time will have slopes that coincide and so they will have the same values. However, early reflections can alter the early decay slope, which will then be different from the full reverberant slope, leading to different values between early decay time and reverberation time. The differences between the two are not usually large,

and it is recommended in concert-hall design that the early decay time should be within 80 per cent of the reverberation time.

Sound Absorption

Sabine's equation states that reverberation time is inversely proportional to sound absorption: the more absorption we introduce into a room, the lower the reverberation time. So what are the mechanisms of sound absorption?

Porous Absorbers

The most common type of sound-absorbing materials are called porous absorbers, and typically they look like the thermal insulation blankets that are installed in lofts. They are manufactured from mineral fibres or elastomeric foams, and are characterized by an open cellular structure of interconnecting pores. The porous surface of these materials allows the sound to penetrate into them, but as the sound waves travel deeper into the material they experience considerable friction against the pores, and the energy of the sound gradually dissipates as it gets converted into heat. The absorption characteristics are dependent on the porosity, density and thickness of the material.

Sound-absorbing materials are characterized by their sound-absorption coefficient, which is the amount of incident sound energy that is absorbed. Sound-absorption coefficients range from 0, which means no absorption, to 1.0, which means 100 per cent of the incident sound energy is absorbed. All materials absorb sound to a certain extent, although hard materials such as brickwork have absorption coefficients that are less than 0.1.

The sound-absorption coefficient of a porous absorber will vary with the frequency of sound, and will generally be lower at low frequencies compared with mid and high frequencies – this is shown in the

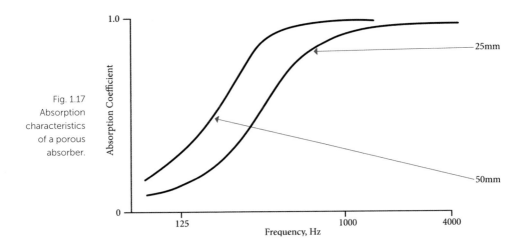

Fig. 1.17 Absorption characteristics of a porous absorber.

curves in Fig. 1.17. The amount of low frequency absorption will depend on the thickness of the material: the thicker the material, the more absorption occurs at low frequencies. This can be seen by comparing the two curves in Fig. 1.17, where the left-hand curve has twice the thickness as the right-hand curve.

The reason that thicker materials are better at absorbing low frequencies is related to the wavelength of sound. When a sound wave is incident on a wall, the air particles at the wall will be at a standstill, but their motion will increase gradually as the distance from the wall increases, until the motion reaches a maximum at a distance of a quarter wavelength. This is where the absorption will be most efficient, and so the thickness of the absorbing material should be at least equivalent to a quarter wavelength. From Fig. 1.17 it is evident that the absorption of a 50mm layer of porous absorber is poor at a frequency of 125Hz, where the wavelength is 2.8m and a quarter wavelength is 0.7m (700mm) – that is, much less than 50mm.

In practice, 50mm-thick porous absorbers are one of the most common thicknesses in general use, and are taken to be effective at around 500Hz and above.

In purely acoustical terms, porous absorbent materials are an effective way of introducing sound absorption into a room. However, from an architectural point of view, the material is not attractive and can be easily damaged, and it is therefore usually faced with a more attractive and robust material. Common facings are board materials, such as timber panelling or plasterboard, which are perforated to enable the sound waves to pass through. Another popular facing for porous absorbers is 'hit-and-miss' timber battens, as shown in Fig. 1.18 on the wall and

Fig. 1.18 A porous absorber faced with 'hit-and-miss' timber battens. (Architect: Allies and Morrison. Photo: Nick Guttridge)

ceiling of a school hall. To ensure that the facing does not unduly impede the passage of sound into the absorbing material, the open area formed by the perforations should be at least 20 per cent of the total area of the boarding.

Panel Absorption

Although porous absorbers are the most common type of sound absorption used in building acoustics, there are other mechanisms of sound absorption that are sometimes used. One of these is panel absorption, where thin timber panelling in a room backed by an air cavity can vibrate in sympathy with an incident sound wave, and thereby absorb energy from that wave. This mechanism depends on the weight of the panel (effectively its thickness) and the depth of the air cavity behind it; these parameters control the frequency range over which the panel is effective. The graph in Fig. 1.19 shows a typical absorption characteristic of a panel absorber. Panel absorbers can be usefully combined with porous absorbers to provide acoustic absorption over the whole audible sound spectrum.

Helmholz or Cavity Resonator

The third type of absorber occurring in architectural acoustics is the so-called Helmholz or cavity resonator. The mechanism can be experienced by blowing across the neck of a bottle, which then produces a single tone. The frequency of this tone depends mainly on the size of the bottle and the length of the neck.

The Helmholz resonator as a sound absorber consists of a cavity that is connected to the surrounding space via a narrow passage or neck. It is very efficient at absorbing sound, but over a very narrow band of frequencies. This is illustrated in Fig. 1.20.

Helmholz resonators are not used widely, but are implemented where there is a need – for example, to reduce reverberation in a certain frequency band. This technique was used in the design of the Queen Elizabeth Hall in London to control low-frequency reverberation. Fig. 1.21 shows the resonators mounted on the walls: the different slot sizes of the resonators are sized to absorb different frequencies.

A more common use of the Helmholz resonator effect is sound-absorbent panelling, which comprises perforated panels backed by an air space.

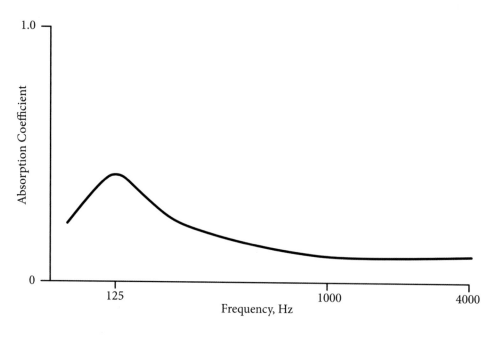

Fig. 1.19
Absorption characteristics of a panel absorber.

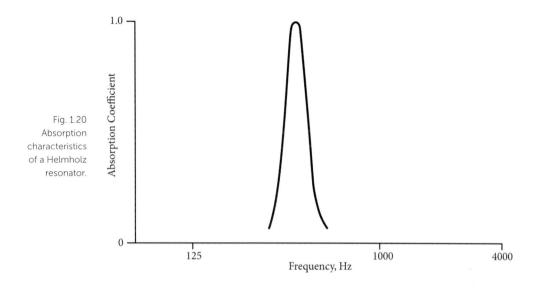

Fig. 1.20
Absorption
characteristics
of a Helmholz
resonator.

Fig. 1.21 Detail
of Helmholz
resonators (a) and
overall view of
Queen Elizabeth
Hall, London (b).

The perforations form the necks of the resonators, and the air space behind forms the cavity of the resonator. It is not usually necessary to divide the cavity into separate compartments by partitions. The cavity is usually filled with mineral wool to extend the absorption to high frequencies. Such resonant absorbers can be designed to be effective at a large range of frequencies, from 100Hz to 4000Hz.

Fig. 1.22 Measuring impulse responses with a gun-shot.

The Finer Details of Reverberation, Impulse Responses and the Importance of Reflection Sequences

It was mentioned earlier that the balance between early and late reflections is fundamental to the quality of the sound that we hear in a space. This balance can be examined by measuring impulse responses, which traditionally were obtained by firing a gunshot, as shown in Fig. 1.22. Typical impulse responses recorded in two spaces with different reverberation times, one about twice as long as the other, are shown in Fig. 1.23.

In the case of speech, it has been shown that reflections arriving within 50 milliseconds (50ms) of the direct sound boost the loudness of the direct sound and are important for ensuring the intelligibility of speech. However, reflections arriving after 50ms, together with reverberation, tend to be detrimental. Therefore it is important to know the fraction of total sound that is useful for aiding the intelligibility of speech. This has led to a measure called the 'early energy fraction', which evaluates the energy in an impulse response in the first 50ms after the direct sound, and compares it with the total energy. The equation for this is as follows:

$$\text{Early energy fraction} = \frac{\text{Early energy (0–50ms)}}{\text{Total energy}}$$

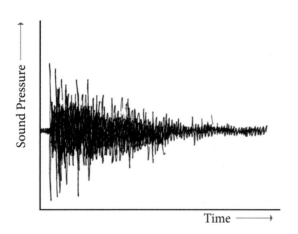

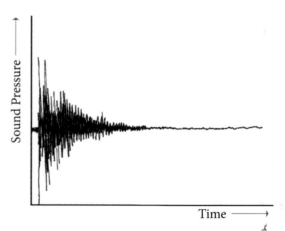

Fig. 1.23 Typical impulse responses in two spaces, with the reverberation time in one about twice as long as the other.

To achieve acceptable levels of the distinctness of speech, the early energy fraction should be at least 0.5; that means at least half of the total energy should be beneficial to the intelligibility of speech.

The relevance of this parameter in the design of spaces for speech is that reflecting surfaces should be located in a room such that they direct early reflections to the listener. A historical example is in churches, where a reflecting panel is located above the pulpit to direct early reflections to the congregation (*see* Chapter 7 for more details).

For music, the balance between early and late sound is critically important. Early reflections will enhance the clarity and distinctness of the music, whilst the late sound will give it a certain fullness, often referred to as reverberance. The ear is thought to respond slightly differently to music signals compared with speech, and so the time window for early reflections is considered to be slightly longer – namely 80ms rather than 50ms. The measure that evaluates the balance between early and late sound is called 'objective clarity', or 'clarity index'; it is expressed in dB by taking the logarithm of the ratio early sound to late sound. The relationship is as follows:

Clarity index, C_{80} (dB)

$$= 10 \log_{10} \frac{\text{Energy arriving within 80ms of direct sound}}{\text{Energy arriving after 80ms}}$$

If the amount of early energy is exactly balanced by the amount of late energy, the ratio of early to late will be unity, and the clarity index will be 0dB. This is considered to be an optimum value for many styles of classical music; generally a range is recommended which is 2dB either side of the optimum value: $-2\text{dB} \leq C_{80} \leq +2\text{dB}$.

So far we have assumed that early reflections are arriving at the listener from various directions. However, research in the 1970s by Marshall and Barron (2001) showed that early reflections arriving at the listener from a lateral direction give rise to a sense of spaciousness – a type of 'surround-sound effect', which is highly desirable when listening to music in an auditorium. Their research led to a measure to evaluate this effect, which is called the 'early lateral energy fraction' or 'lateral efficiency' (LE). This measure is expressed by the following relationship:

$$\text{Lateral efficiency} = \frac{\text{Energy arriving laterally within 80ms of direct sound}}{\text{Total energy arriving within 80ms of direct sound}}$$

The implications of this effect have been far-reaching in the design of concert halls. In essence, to maximize the feeling of spaciousness in a hall when listening to music, the early lateral reflections arriving at listening positions should be strong relative to other reflections. To achieve this, halls should either be narrow in shape or should include internal surfaces to produce these early lateral reflections.

The optimum range of values for lateral efficiency is quoted as $0.1 \leq \text{LE} \leq 0.35$.

The final measure to be mentioned which is in common usage in room acoustic design is 'total sound level', which is also called 'strength' and has the symbol G. This measure is related to the loudness of sound, and represents the total energy in the impulse response. It is formally defined as the total energy in the impulse response relative to the energy of the direct sound at a distance of 10m, and is quoted in dB. Values in concert halls depend on the size of the hall; typically values are around 6dB for medium-sized halls (1,000 seats), and around 3 to 4dB for large halls (2,000 seats).

Loudness is a very important attribute in listening to music, and it can be challenging to achieve sufficient levels in large halls, so it is important to design these halls to obtain sufficient loudness.

Implications for Design

In terms of designing rooms for speech and music, reverberation time remains the most important parameter, and it is crucial for the space to have sufficient volume in relation to the total acoustic absorption. This absorption is usually dominated by the audience and seating, which is a well documented quantity: it has led to the rule of thumb for designing concert halls which is that the required volume can be estimated by providing $10m^3$ ($13yd^3$) per audience person. For theatres, it is about half that value, namely 4 to $5m^3$ (5 to $6.5yd^3$) per person.

We also know that reverberation is not the total answer. The sequence of early reflections and their balance with reverberation are key to obtaining acoustic excellence. To achieve the optimum sequence of reflections, it is necessary to shape the geometry of the room to direct early reflections throughout the seating areas, and to ensure that the delays of these reflections are within the appropriate time windows.

Therefore room acoustic design needs to take into account three fundamental factors, namely room volume, total acoustic absorption and room geometry, in order to provide the right reflection sequence.

Chapter Two

Opera Houses and Concert Halls (Pre-Twentieth Century)

IN REVIEWING THE EVOLUTION OF AUDITORIUM design and the associated acoustic qualities of auditoria, it is useful to start with the Greek amphitheatre and see how this has developed first into enclosed theatres, then opera houses and then concert halls. A major step change in acoustic design occurred at the turn of the twentieth century when the physicist, Wallace Clement Sabine, proposed his theory of reverberation: therefore halls designed in the twentieth and twenty-first centuries are dealt with in a separate chapter. This chapter deals with auditorium design before Sabine's work, where the design process was based largely on empiricism.

The Classical Greek Theatre

One of the best examples of classical Greek theatre, which was introduced in the previous chapter, and which is still in use today, is the theatre at Epidaurus in the Peloponnese. It was built around 300BC and has a huge audience capacity of around 14,000. It has

developed a reputation of having wonderful acoustics, although even today, scientists have not been able to confirm that there is anything exceptional about the acoustics of the space.

Nevertheless, Epidaurus does have good acoustics for speech, and this can still be experienced today by speakers who can project their voice (the ancient Greeks, in fact, wore masks during performances which amplified their voices to some extent). There are three principal reasons why the acoustics at Epidaurus are good for speech. First, the location is very quiet so that disturbance by background noise is minimized. Secondly, the seating rake is very steep, over 26 degrees, so that the sound travelling from speaker to listener has a clear, unobstructed path. Thirdly, the stage – or *orchestra* as it is correctly called – is made of stone, which is a good reflector of sound and directs a strong reflection towards the audience: this strengthens the direct sound and makes it louder. Even this reflected sound has a clear path from speaker to listener because of the steep seating rake; this is illustrated in Fig. 2.1.

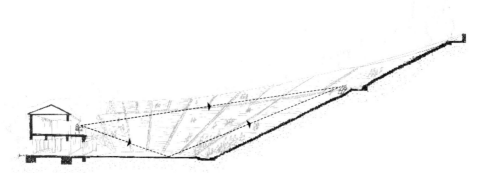

Fig. 2.1 Section of Epidaurus showing direct and reflected sound.

There is one minor acoustical problem with this theatre: namely, that the seats at the sides have rather weaker sound because of the directionality of the human voice. The Greeks were aware of this, and reserved these seats for particular groups of people – latecomers, foreigners and pregnant women!

Teatro Olimpico, Vicenza

The classical amphitheatre design of the Greeks was adopted during the Renaissance, but was covered over with a roof, forming an enclosed space. A classic example is the Teatro Olimpico at Vicenza by the renowned architect Andrea Palladio, which was completed in 1585. Roofing over the *cavea*, as the audience area is called, created a multitude of additional reflections, causing the sound to reverberate around the space. Recent measurements of the reverberation time in the unoccupied room indicated a value close to three seconds at mid frequencies, with a shorter value of around two seconds at bass frequencies (Bonsi 2012). Although these values will decrease when an audience is present, they are not well suited to speech but are rather better for music, although the shorter value at bass frequencies would be perceived as lack of *warmth* in the sound. Furthermore, the semi-circular geometry on plan, as shown in Fig. 2.2 – which effectively does not have sidewalls – means that there were few lateral reflections, which are now considered to be important for enhancing the quality of music.

In essence, the Teatro Olimpico is better suited to music than speech, although even for music it is not ideal. However, there is evidence to suggest that the acoustics were suited to the early writing styles exemplified by Gabrieli's choruses (Orazio and Nannini, *Acoustics*, 2019).

It is interesting to note that a similar plan geometry was adopted in the nineteenth century for a now famous auditorium in acoustical history: the lecture theatre at the Fogg Art Museum in Cambridge, Massachusetts, in which Wallace Clement

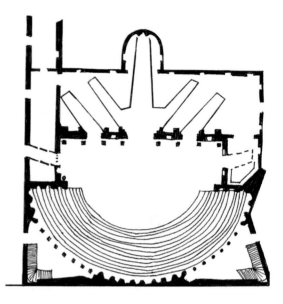

Fig. 2.2 Plan of Teatro Olimpico.

Sabine carried out his pioneering work on the theory of room acoustics (*see* Chapter 1).

The Baroque Opera House

Early Italian Opera Houses

The classical amphitheatre design of the Greeks was again adopted for the design of early opera houses. The beginnings of opera were in Florence in the sixteenth century, where singing and dancing were staged on festive occasions in courtly surroundings (a full description of the development of the opera house is given by Forsyth (1985)). The operas written at this time recreated classical Greek theatre, and the venues in which they were performed were derived from the Greek amphitheatre form.

The Teatro Farnese in Parma (1610) is in the form of an amphitheatre but with elongated sides that form a 'U' shape (*see* Fig. 2.3); the central area was regularly used as an extension of the stage, sometimes for spectacular enactments such as mock sea battles. The architect, Giovan Battista Aleotti, introduced a major new element in his design: the proscenium

Fig. 2.3 Teatro Farnese. (Photo: Toni Spagone, Alamy)

arch. This feature effectively separated the real world from theatrical fiction. As well as providing visual separation, it was acoustically beneficial in providing early reflections from the stage and orchestra.

Venice at this time was undergoing a great blossoming in renaissance music, and welcomed the arrival of opera, building the first theatre specifically for opera, the Teatro San Cassiano in 1637. Forsyth describes the new opera house as having tiers around the walls to accommodate as many people as possible because the venue intended to be profit-making; also, the orchestra was placed for the first time in front of the stage.

A particularly important early Venetian opera house was the Teatro SS. Giovanni e Paolo, because it was the first horseshoe-shaped Italian baroque opera house; it is shown in plan in Fig. 2.4. It was completed for opera performances in 1654, and is a seminal design that has influenced opera house design to this day. The walls were lined with five tiers of boxes, with additional seating on the 'U'-shaped floor to accommodate as large a paying audience as possible.

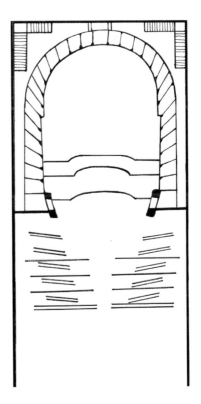

Fig. 2.4 Plan of Teatro SS. Giovanni e Paolo.

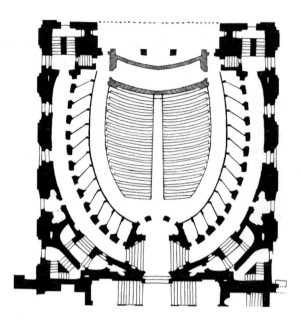

Fig. 2.5 Plan of Teatro Regio.

In addition to the horseshoe- and 'U'-shaped opera houses, the truncated ellipse became a common form. An eminent example of this form was the Teatro Regio in Turin (1738–1740), which was acclaimed for both its architecture and its acoustics (Forsyth, 1985). A plan is shown in Fig. 2.5.

In acoustical terms, the three plan forms of opera houses described above – namely horseshoe, 'U'-shaped and truncated ellipse – have the potential for providing good, sometimes excellent, acoustics. The fundamental characteristic of these houses is the main auditorium volume, which is surrounded by tiers of boxes; the balcony fronts of these boxes reflect sound, whereas the box openings absorb sound. The main volume, if sufficiently large, produces ample reverberation, and the balcony fronts produce early reflections, which can enhance clarity and intimacy. However, these acoustical attributes are only perceived by the audience in the stalls and those in the front rows of the boxes; those seated further back in the boxes experience an increasingly remote sound the further back they are. So boxes are not particularly good in acoustical design terms.

The curved geometry of these opera houses can cause some focusing, although the heavy ornamentation, sometimes coupled with draperies, tended to reduce the severity of this effect.

The Galli-Bibiena Family

The most famous architects of opera houses in this era were the Galli-Bibiena family, who dominated opera house design for over a century, starting around 1700. The key feature of their designs was the bell-shaped plan, rather than the horseshoe and its related forms. This shape does not appear to have any particular merit acoustically, and was probably adopted for optimizing sightlines (Barron 2010).

Although the Galli-Bibienas did not write about acoustics, a contemporary author, Francesco Algarotti, based some of his writings on their designs. He agreed that masonry should be used for the main structure, which also prevented fire, and that timber linings should be used internally to 'equalize' the sound – in other words, to control the reverberation at low frequencies. He also noted that flat walls made the voice too 'sharp', while a room with tapestries made the voice too 'silent'. He recommended that the rooms should be lined with timber to make the voice loud and pleasant (Orazio and Nannini, *Acoustics*, 2019).

One of the most outstanding designs by the Galli-Bibienas was the Markgrafliches Opernhaus in Bayreuth, the interior of which was carried out by Giuseppe Galli-Bibiena and his son Carlo; it opened in 1747. It is still in existence today, and was fully refurbished in 2018; views of the opera house are shown in Fig. 2.6. The design is highly ornate in the Italian late baroque style, and has the signature bell-shaped plan. This heavy ornamentation has the acoustical advantage of producing

Fig. 2.6
Markgrafliches
Opernhaus.
(Photo: David
Leventi)

a highly diffuse sound field, which minimizes any focusing and ensures uniformity over the seating area. The auditorium is an intimate space seating 520 distributed over a flat stalls floor, a gallery, and three tiers of loges.

The design approach of the Galli-Bibienas was highly influential in the design of other opera houses, a good example being the Residenz Theatre in Munich by a Belgian architect, François Cuvilliés, which was completed in 1753; it has four tiers of boxes and a 'U'-shaped plan, shown in Fig. 2.7. The interior design is in the rococo style rather than the baroque, which also provides generous ornamentation to diffuse the sound. The theatre was bombed in World War ll but recreated in the 1950s, and further modernized between 2004 and 2008; it has been renamed the Cuvilliés Theatre.

As opera-going in Italy became more popular, the size of opera houses increased. The largest at this time was the Teatro San Carlo in Naples, which was completed in 1737. The design was based on a horseshoe plan with six tiers of boxes and around 1,400 seats; a plan is shown in Fig. 2.8.

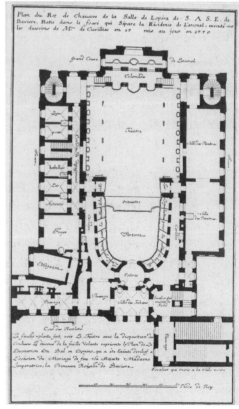

Fig. 2.7 Plan of the Residenz Theatre. (Bayerische Staatsbibliothek)

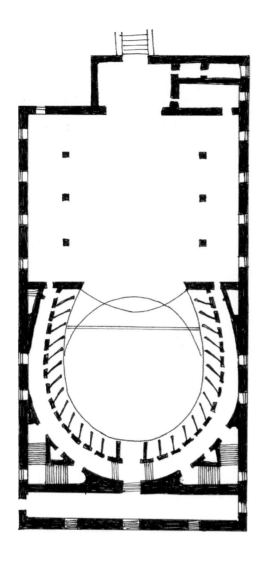

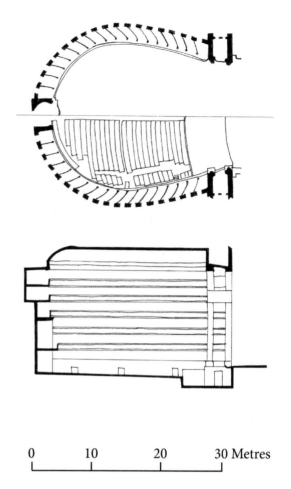

Fig. 2.9 Plan and section of Teatro alla Scala.

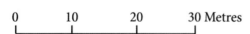

Fig. 2.8 Plan of Teatro San Carlo, Naples.

Teatro alla Scala, Milan

The most famous opera house in Italy was built some forty years later in 1778: the Teatro alla Scala in Milan. It is very large in comparison with earlier houses, seating 2,800 with seven tiers of boxes; the plan shape is a classical horseshoe, as shown in Fig. 2.9.

In acoustical terms, La Scala is considered one of the world's leading opera houses. Its characteristics are similar to other baroque opera houses in that the acoustics are best on the main floor and at the front of the boxes, while those listeners further back in the boxes receive a poorer sound. The openings to the boxes are only 45 per cent of the height of a tier, which restricts the incident sound; furthermore this sound decreases rapidly with distance as the boxes are acoustically absorbent. By contrast, the balcony fronts reflect a substantial proportion of incident sound back into the main volume, which enhances the clarity and intimacy for listeners on the main floor.

La Scala was bombed during World War ll but was repaired in 1946, and underwent a major refurbishment in 2004. A view of the auditorium is shown in Fig. 2.10.

Fig. 2.10 Teatro alla Scala, Milan. (Photo: Anne-Marie Palmer, Alamy)

French Opera Houses

In the latter half of the eighteenth century, France became more influential in opera house design; a particular feature was the replacement of boxes with galleries. An important example of this development is the Grand Theatre in Bordeaux of 1780, which has a balcony and two tiers of mini galleries; it seats 1,200. The auditorium is a very intimate space both visually and acoustically; this has been achieved by adopting a plan shape that approximates a truncated circle (Fig. 2.11) – the distance from the stage front to the furthest seat is only 20m. The combination of open galleries and short distances between audience and stage produces an intimate acoustic experience.

English Opera Houses

In England, many operas were performed in the Theatre Royal, Drury Lane, although this venue was a playhouse, not an opera house according to the Licensing Act imposed during the Interregnum when the puritan Oliver Cromwell ruled. A description of the Drury Lane theatre is given in the chapter on

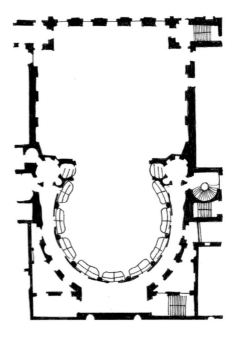

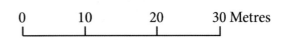

Fig. 2.11 Plan of the Grand Theatre, Bordeaux.

theatres. Covent Garden Theatre was also officially a playhouse at this time, but was remodelled as an opera house in 1847 when the Licensing Act was repealed. Unfortunately this version of the opera house lasted less than ten years as it was destroyed by fire during a ball in 1856. It was rebuilt in 1858 by the architect E.M. Barry, who adopted the classic horseshoe form surmounted by a shallow dome with four levels of boxes, including a gallery. The plan and section are shown in Fig. 2.12.

The arrangement of open galleries with an extensive upper gallery provides audiences at Covent Garden with more egalitarian acoustics than in the classic Italian houses, although there are some differences between seating areas. The most favourable acoustics are at the front of the upper gallery, which receives a useful ceiling reflection. The reasonably small distance between opposite balconies means that the balcony fronts provide useful early reflections to a majority of the seats, and provide the listener with a clear enveloping sound – *see* Fig. 2.13.

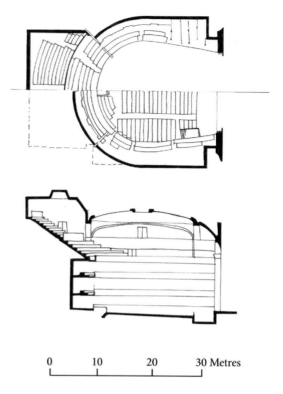

0   10   20   30 Metres

Fig. 2.12 Plan and section of Covent Garden Opera House.

Fig. 2.13 Covent Garden Opera House.

As in many opera houses, the sound in the stalls can sometimes lack clarity as there is no line-of-sight to the pit, and the acoustic quality under balcony overhangs can lack reverberance. Before the refurbishment in the 1990s (*see* below), overall the acoustics were considered to be good, with a clear sound, but lacking in reverberance and warmth.

The refurbishment was carried out over a three-year period with the house reopening in 1999; the architects were Dixon Jones, with acoustic advice by Arup. The main aim was to improve the sightlines and enhance the acoustics whilst preserving the heritage aspects of the space. The changes involved new flooring, walls and box partitioning, and work on the amphitheatre ceiling with a view to reducing low-frequency absorption. Carpeting was removed to reduce mid- and high-frequency absorption, and the new seating was carefully calibrated in an acoustic test chamber to ensure an appropriate sound absorption characteristic. The size of the opening to the amphitheatre was enlarged, creating extra volume to contribute to an increase in the reverberation time, whilst at the same time increasing the audience capacity to 2,366. The stalls rake was increased to improve sightlines, which also improves 'sound lines', and the box dividers were reduced for the same reason.

Following these changes, final acoustic tests in the unoccupied auditorium showed that a modest but significant increase had occurred in the reverberation time to 1.3 seconds at mid-frequencies, with an uplift in the bass to 1.5 seconds (Newton 2001). This increase helps to enhance the reverberance and warmth of the sound, which was noted to be lacking prior to the refurbishment.

After the construction of E.M. Barry's Covent Garden Opera House of 1858, the next major opera house to be built was the Paris Opera by architect Charles Garnier, which was opened in 1875. The architectural design was highly ornate and opulent, and followed the traditional horseshoe plan shape with four tiers of boxes seating 2,000. The design incorporated elements of Palladian classicism and baroque styles, but also incorporated modern building techniques such as the use of an iron structural frame. Its acoustic design is interesting in that Garnier professed to know nothing about acoustics and did not follow any acoustic principles, and yet the outcome has proved to be successful. This is probably because the design adhered to a traditional opera house form, which had worked satisfactorily in the past.

The horseshoe plan shape has remained the preferred shape for opera houses for at least 200 years, with a few exceptions, and remains popular in the twenty-first century.

The Festspielhaus, Bayreuth

One of the exceptions is the Festspielhaus in Bayreuth, whose design evolved from radical thinking between the architect Gottfried Semper and the opera composer Richard Wagner.

Wagner disliked the social stratification and poor sightlines of baroque theatres, and developed a wedge-shaped auditorium with a single tier of steeply raked seating, which provided an egalitarian arrangement with good sightlines for an audience of 1,800. A plan of the auditorium is shown in Fig. 2.14.

The acoustics turned out to be appropriate for Wagner's operas – a long reverberation time of 1.55 seconds, and a muted orchestral sound due to a large, specially designed orchestra pit that was covered over with a hood on the audience side. This partially enclosed pit reduced the loudness of the orchestral sound but also changed its balance, high frequency sounds being suppressed relative to bass sounds. The intention of the hood was to visually conceal the orchestra, but it also made it sound more mysterious, and at the same time, it helped the balance between singers and orchestra. The enhanced bass sound could have resulted in the auditorium

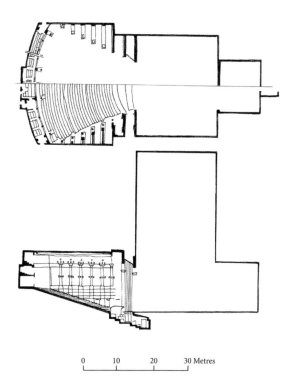

0   10   20   30 Metres

Fig. 2.14 Plan and section of the Festspielhaus, Bayreuth.

sounding 'boomy', but this effect was controlled by chance by the low frequency absorption of the thin wall panelling and a lightweight timber ceiling.

Although the seating plan is fan-shaped, the walls of the auditorium are parallel, and piers projecting from the sidewalls define the seating area and provide some useful sound diffusion. The rear wall of the fan is curved, which could have resulted in a disturbing echo, but fortunately this was avoided by incorporating two galleries for special guests, at the request of the chief sponsor King Ludwig ll. A view of the auditorium is shown in Fig. 2.15.

Despite challenges in realizing his opera house, Wagner, collaborating with new architect Otto Bruckwald, finally managed to complete the building in 1876.

Fig. 2.15 The Festspielhaus, Bayreuth.

Concert Halls

Haydnsaal, Esterházy Castle, Austria

By contrast with opera houses, concert halls evolved from the acoustically intimate rooms of the eighteenth century, such as the Haydnsaal at the Esterházy Castle of Eisenstadt. Haydn became assistant Kapellmeister to the Esterházy family in 1761 and remained in their service for forty years, during which time he composed many of his works.

The Haydnsaal, which was originally a banqueting room, was created in the castle during a baroque building phase between 1663 and 1672. The form of the room is rectangular, with a narrow width of 14.7m (48ft) and a high ceiling of 12.4m (40.7ft), which gives an ample volume of 6,800m³ (8,894yd³); it seats around 400 (*see* Fig. 2.16). The reverberation time when it is occupied is 1.7 seconds at mid-frequencies with a substantial rise in the bass; this is quite long for the size of room, and comparable with much larger modern concert halls seating 2,000 or more. The long reverberation time, coupled with strong reflections from the narrow side walls, has the ingredients for producing an intense enveloping sound, and it is suggested that Haydn was aware of this desirable effect (Barron 2010).

Musikvereinssaal, Vienna

Intimate concert rooms such as the Haydnsaal were succeeded in the later nineteenth century by larger and more reverberant halls such as the Musikvereinssaal in Vienna and the Concertgebouw in Amsterdam. The reason for this increase in size is that the general public wanted to attend these musical concerts, which until then had tended to be the exclusive prerogative of the aristocracy, and the public were willing to pay an entrance fee.

Fig. 2.16 The Haydnsaal at Eisenstadt. (Bildagentur GmbH/Alamy)

The Grosser Musikvereinssaal, built in 1872, is regarded as one of the world's best concert halls for classical and romantic music. Music played in this hall is heard with a high degree of clarity, together with a fullness of tone (often called reverberance), and with ample loudness. There is also a feeling of being intimately involved with the musical performance, and being enveloped by the sound.

Characteristic architectural features are a narrow width (20m) and a high ceiling (18m), with intricate surface ornamentation. These features are illustrated in the three images in Fig. 2.17.

The design of the Musikvereinssaal is seminal in that many nineteenth-century halls were built in this shape: this form has become known as the 'shoebox' shape. These shoebox-shaped halls had similar characteristics to the Musikvereinssaal and were generally acoustically successful. The design of the Musikvereinssaal, carried out 150 years ago, did not involve specialist acoustic advice – its acoustical success is due to architectural empiricism and good fortune.

Royal Albert Hall, London

One large capacity hall, built at the same time as the Musikvereinssaal, is the Royal Albert Hall with 5,000 seats; it was opened in 1871. The architect, Captain Francis Fowkes, had never designed a concert hall before, although he was noted for designing a portable rubber bath for officers!

The Royal Albert Hall developed a reputation soon after it opened for having a serious acoustical fault: an echo from the ceiling. Not only did this echo suffer a long delay (about a quarter of a second), but it was

Fig. 2.17 The Musikvereinssaal in Vienna: (a) auditorium, (b) stage, (c) decorative statues.

Fig. 2.17 *Continued.*

focused by the dome and therefore relatively loud. At the time, a saying developed among concert goers that you could have two concerts for the price of one! Early attempts to reduce the echo involved hanging a huge cloth 'velarium' under the dome, as shown in Fig. 2.18, but this was not very successful.

It was not until 1968 that the echo problem was investigated thoroughly using gunshots and a bassoon as sound sources, together with a highly directional microphone. The photograph in Fig. 2.19 shows the acoustic testing taking place. The investigation resulted in the suspension of 135 convex saucers, often referred to as 'mushrooms', beneath the dome, which helped to scatter the incident sound before it reached the dome. The upper surface of the saucers was acoustically absorbent so that residual sound reflected from the dome was absorbed on its way down.

During the refurbishment of the hall in 1996, the echo was investigated again in even further

Fig. 2.18 The Royal Albert Hall with cloth 'velarium' suspended below the ceiling.

Fig. 2.19 Acoustic tests in the Royal Albert Hall.

Fig. 2.20 Suspended 'mushrooms' in the Royal Albert Hall.

detail with the help of a 1:12-scale acoustic model. A number of new options were proposed to suppress the echo, including the installation of a glass velarium, together with some sound-absorbing and diffusing elements at lower levels. However, the most economical option proved to be the retention of the 'mushrooms', although they were reduced in number to eighty-five and reconfigured in a denser arrangement – sometimes called the 'condensed mushroom' configuration! This new arrangement, shown in Fig. 2.20, was completed in 2001 and has been the most successful in suppressing the notorious echo.

Concertgebouw, Amsterdam

The Royal Albert Hall is an exceptional concert hall both in terms of its size and shape. When investigating the possible designs for a new hall for Amsterdam in the 1880s, the backers considered that the 'shoebox' shape was the most reliable in terms of acoustics, and used as their exemplars the Neues Gewandhaus in Leipzig (destroyed in World War ll), the Musikvereinssaal in Vienna, and the Tonhalle in Düsseldorf (also destroyed in World War ll).

The brief for the architectural competition specified an audience size of 2,000, an orchestra size of 120 musicians and space for 500 choir members. The competition was won by Dolf van Gendt, even though the width of his hall was significantly wider than the exemplars: 29m (95ft) compared to around 20m (65ft). Other features of his design were a very large stage for orchestra and choir, with steep risers and a rear stage wall with rounded ends. It had a high ceiling of 17.5m (57ft) that was heavily coffered, and there was a single balcony around three sides of the hall; a plan and section of the auditorium is shown in Fig. 2.21.

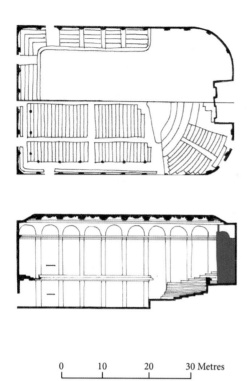

Fig. 2.21 Plan and section of the Concertgebouw, Amsterdam.

Fig. 2.22 The
Concertgebouw,
Amsterdam.

The hall was completed in 1888, and the acoustical reputation it developed over the first few years was poor. The main criticism was that the hall resonated too strongly, and also that the brass overpowered the strings. The arrival of a new conductor in 1895, Willem Mengelberg, changed the style of orchestral performances to better suit the long reverberation, and the acoustical reputation was greatly enhanced. He also had the stage rebuilt with a shallower slope, which improved the balance between the brass and the strings. Increasing the size of the audience helped to reduce the excessive reverberation, and the later introduction of absorbent seats further helped this.

Acoustically, the hall differs slightly from the strict shoebox halls such as the Musikvereinssaal; this is partly due to its larger width. This means that early reflections are not as strong in the main body of the seating, which reduces clarity in favour of reverberance. The sound in the balcony is considered to be clear and well balanced (Barron 2010). If the performance is not a choral concert, the choir seats can be occupied by audience – these seats can be seen in

the view of the concert hall in Fig. 2.22. This disposition of part of the audience behind the orchestra has parallels with the surround halls of today (described in the following chapter).

Recent renovations, with acoustical advice by the firm Peutz, were carried out between 1985 and 2002. These were aimed at preserving the acclaimed acoustics of the hall: the measured reverberation time was 2.4 seconds when unoccupied, and predicted to be 2.1 seconds when occupied (Vercammen 2019). This is in the preferred range for symphonic music, but towards the higher end. Interestingly Vercammen predicted that with a small ensemble on stage and an audience of only 300, the reverberation time in the original hall would have been 4 seconds, so it is not surprising that the acoustics in the early days were heavily criticized.

Now that the reverberation time has been controlled, the Concertgebouw is considered to be one of the three best concert halls in the world, the other two being the Musikvereinssaal and the Boston Symphony Hall. The Concertgebouw is particularly suited to performances of the late Romantic repertoire, for which it is highly acclaimed.

Chapter Three

Opera Houses and Concert Halls (Twentieth to Twenty-First Centuries)

A MAJOR STEP CHANGE IN ACOUSTIC DESIGN occurred at the turn of the twentieth century, when the physicist Wallace Clement Sabine proposed his theory of reverberation. His equation for calculating reverberation time is seductively simple, and has profoundly influenced auditorium design in the twentieth and twenty-first centuries.

Sabine's theory helped to dispel much confusion in acoustics, which still existed even at the beginning of the twentieth century. Such confusion is illustrated by an essay written by the eminent Viennese architect, Adolf Loos (1912), entitled *Das Mysterium der Akustik*, in which he proposed that concert halls become acoustically excellent when fine music played in them is gradually absorbed by the walls. In the mortar, he said, live the sounds of great composers. The music of our symphony orchestras and the voices of singers impregnate the building materials, causing mysterious changes in the molecular structure, as in the wood of old violins. But brass instruments, he warned, had a bad effect, and military music played in a fine hall could ruin its acoustics within a week. For the same reason, opera houses have poor acoustics on the side where the brass players sit!

By contrast with Adolf Loos' tenuous hypothesizing, Sabine pursued an objective approach, having proposed the concept of reverberation time, which is based on the prolongation of sound in a room; in subjective terms it is often referred to as reverberance. Sabine showed that it is linked to acoustic quality – short reverberation times give high clarity and little reverberance; conversely, long reverberation times give less clarity and more reverberance.

Sabine's work was greatly expanded in the second half of the twentieth century, when an active period of acoustics research in several countries led to a deeper understanding of auditorium acoustics, and consequently to new design concepts.

Sabine and Boston Symphony Hall

Boston Symphony Hall was the first concert hall to benefit from the advice and acoustical theories of Sabine. In deciding what the acoustical quality and reverberation time should be, Sabine referred to two example halls: the Old Boston Music Hall, and the Neues Gewandhaus in Leipzig. He did not consider the Old Boston Music Hall to be very good acoustically, and concentrated more on the Neues Gewandhaus.

The seating capacity of the Neues Gewandhaus was 1,560, and for the new hall Sabine needed to increase this by 70 per cent to 2,600. He made it clear that the design was not simply a matter of proportionately increasing the dimensions, and he therefore carried out careful calculations according to his theory to define length, width and height. He predicted that the reverberation time for the new hall would be 2.3 seconds, very similar to the

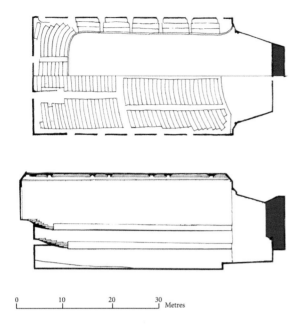

0   10   20   30 Metres

Fig. 3.1 Plan and section of Boston Symphony Hall.

Neues Gewandhaus (the actual reverberation time when the hall is occupied is 1.8 seconds, as Sabine underestimated seating absorption).

Sabine also noted that the length of the Boston Hall would be about the same as the Neues Gewandhaus, and although the orchestra was a bit further from the rear wall, the support from the stage enclosure would compensate for the loudness (Sabine 1922). The hall was built in line with Sabine's instructions, and opened in 1900. It is shown in plan and section in Fig. 3.1.

The hall, which is a classic shoebox, has come to be regarded as one of the three best concert halls in the world. Beranek (2004) describes the sound as 'clear, live, warm, brilliant and loud, without being overly loud'. A view of the hall is shown in Fig. 3.2.

Fig. 3.2 Boston Symphony Hall. (Photo: Alamy)

Other Early Twentieth-Century Halls

Unfortunately, Sabine's work was not widely disseminated in the first part of the twentieth century, and most halls built in this period did not benefit from it. The attention of architects after World War l was focused on the Modern Movement, with its embracing of minimalism and its rejection of ornamentation exemplified by the Beaux Arts and Neoclassical architectural styles of the nineteenth century. This new style was reflected in the design of concert halls of that period, where the architecture was dominant and the acoustical input to the design was marginal. In fact, although Sabine's work was published, little reference was made to it.

In North America there was a school of thought that considered concert halls should be like outdoor music pavilions, where reflected sound was only provided for the musicians. This concept was set out by the American acoustician, F.R. Watson, who proposed two rules:

- Provide a stage with suitable reflecting surfaces so that performers can 'hear themselves'
- Design the auditorium for listening so that the reflected sound will be reduced to be comparable with outdoor conditions

Watson argued that reflected sound was the cause of acoustic defects in auditoria and should therefore be avoided (Forsyth 1985). Of course, this philosophy would not be acceptable with present-day knowledge. However, several major auditoria were built in line with Watson's philosophy, including the Eastman Theatre in Rochester, New York, and the Severance Hall in Cleveland. These halls were characterized by heavy drapery and carpets, and had relatively short reverberation times – 1.5 seconds in the case of Severance Hall. They were not well suited to orchestral music, and were refurbished in the second half of the twentieth century to improve their acoustics (Beranek 2004).

In this period there was an emphasis on increasing audience sizes, and to ensure that audiences were not too far from the stage, the fan-shape plan became popular. This approach mirrored to some extent the development of cinema design. These fan-shaped halls were characterized by a low volume with respect to audience size, and were often overly acoustically absorbent, resulting in a low reverberation time.

There are also other acoustical problems associated with fan-shaped halls. The rear wall is typically curved, which causes focusing of sound. The larger width at the back means that seats in the centre have few early reflections, and in particular there is a lack of early lateral reflections, as most of the reflections from the angled walls are directed towards the rear. This lack of early lateral reflections means that the feeling of being surrounded by the sound is weak.

A different approach to acoustical design was developed in Europe at this time. It is epitomized by the design of the Salle Pleyel in Paris, which was led acoustically by Gustav Lyon. Lyon had determined that reflections are a key component of the transmission of sound, and that a useful reflection should arrive within 1/15th second (67ms) after the direct sound. He then proceeded to profile the ceiling of the hall to reflect sound from the stage to the various sections of the audience with this criterion in mind; the profile became a cylindrical parabola, as shown in Fig. 3.3. A view of the hall is shown in Fig. 3.4.

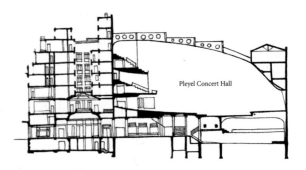

Pleyel Concert Hall

Fig. 3.3 Section of Salle Pleyel, Paris.

Fig. 3.4 Salle Pleyel (prior to the 2004–2006 refurbishment).

The result of this design is that nearly all the sound which is incident on the ceiling is directed on to the absorbent audience; the absorption was further increased by carpeting and other sound-absorbing materials. The result was a loud, clear sound but lacking in reverberation and reflections from other directions, so it was not well suited to musical performances. The hall has since undergone a number of refurbishments in recent times, which have improved the acoustics.

Another hall based on this concept is the Konserthus in Gothenburg in Sweden, which opened in 1935. It suffers from a short reverberation time and also from a lack of spatial sound.

Halls in the Second Half of The Twentieth Century

A new era in concert-hall design started after World War ll; this was heralded in the UK by the Royal Festival Hall.

The Royal Festival Hall

The project to build a new concert hall, the Royal Festival Hall, as part of the Festival of Britain in 1951, was a great opportunity to create a brand new venue after the austerity of the war years. There was also a pressing need for a new concert hall, as the Queen's Hall had been destroyed by bombing during the war. The key architects involved in the design were amongst the most outstanding practitioners of that time, namely Robert Matthew and Leslie Martin, and they were joined by the leading acoustician in England, Hope Bagnall, who worked in collaboration with acousticians at the Building Research Station.

It was decided at an early stage for the hall to have a large seating capacity, and a figure of 3,000 was set, although some of the design team would have preferred it even larger – nevertheless the hall remains one of the largest concert halls in Europe.

The choice of plan shape was fundamental, and it would have been easy to follow the fashion of fan-shaped or 'cinema-style' halls that had become popular in the earlier part of the century. However, Bagnall felt that the cross-reflections that occur in the traditionally shaped shoebox halls were important for acoustical quality, in particular 'fullness of tone', and so he promoted a rectangular-shaped hall. His inklings about the importance of cross-reflections were later proved accurate by the work of Marshall and Barron (2001).

Having chosen a rectangular plan shape, it was necessary to bring the audience as close as possible to the stage, certainly not further than 40m (130ft), and so a large balcony was incorporated into the design. It was understood that seats at the rear of the balcony would receive weaker sound, and to compensate for this, the ceiling was shaped to direct sound from the stage to the balcony. A canopy above the stage was also shaped and positioned to direct sound towards the rear seats, as well as to provide some reflected sound to the orchestra to give them support. A plan and long section of the hall section are shown in Fig. 3.5.

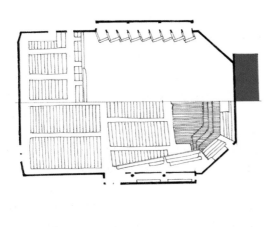

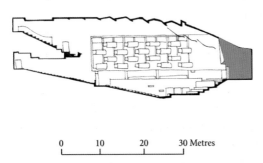

0   10   20   30 Metres

Fig. 3.5 Plan and section of the Royal Festival Hall.

The only reliable objective parameter in concert-hall acoustics at that time was reverberation time, and a target was set for a value of 2.2 seconds, which was considered suitable for a concert hall for symphonic music. However, as the design progressed, it became clear that this target could not be achieved, as the volume relative to the number of seats was too small. It was not possible to increase the volume by raising the roof owing to structural limitations, and it was not acceptable to reduce the number of seats. The target reverberation time was therefore lowered to 1.7 seconds, which was considered reasonable.

On completion of the hall, the measured reverberation time was 1.5 seconds, which was significantly below the desired target, with the result that the hall gained a reputation for high clarity of sound but a lack of 'fullness of tone' or reverberance. A view of the concert hall is shown in Fig. 3.6. One of the reasons for the shortfall was that the ceiling construction was considerably lighter than specified, and therefore absorbed too much bass sound. This reputation became consolidated after a number of years, and the management decided that it had to be corrected.

There were three options for making a correction: firstly, to raise the roof; secondly to reduce the number of seats; and thirdly to install an electronic enhancement system. Raising the roof would have been extremely expensive, reducing the number of seats was not economically acceptable, and so it was decided to adopt the electronic system.

The proposed electronic system was developed at the Building Research Station by Peter Parkin and his colleagues. It involved installing a large number of channels (eighty-nine) in the ceiling, where each channel comprised a microphone, an amplifier and a loudspeaker (Parkin 1965). The principle of the system was to harness the feedback or 'ringing' effect of amplification systems, where the gain of the amplifier determined the increase in reverberation but had to be carefully controlled to avoid sound coloration and possible feedback; the system became known as 'assisted resonance'. Each microphone was contained

Fig. 3.6 The Royal Festival Hall before the 2007 refurbishment.

in a Helmholz resonator, a small device shaped like a wine bottle, whose resonance frequency could be adjusted with a movable piston, as shown in Fig. 3.7.

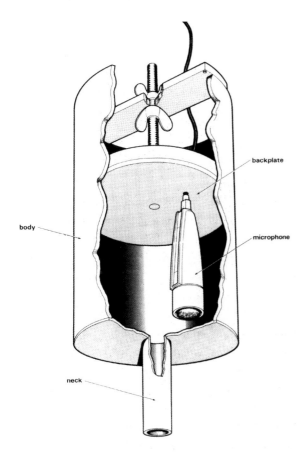

Fig. 3.7 Adjustable Helmholz resonator (after P.H. Parkin).

Ironically, these resonators were originally installed in the ceiling to reduce reverberation if it was excessive – now they were to be used for the opposite effect: to increase the reverberation. The resonators were tuned to different frequencies, each 3Hz apart, so that a wide band of low frequencies was covered, from 70Hz to 340Hz.

This system was trialled in 1964 without informing the public, and proved very successful in increasing the reverberation time. It was subsequently made permanent, and extended by introducing more channels to increase the frequency range from 58Hz to 700Hz. The increase in reverberation time is shown in Fig. 3.8, where it is evident that the uplift at low frequencies is substantial, and the resultant values are close to the original intentions for the hall.

Performers and listeners alike noted a more reverberant and warmer sound, and there were few objections to the introduction of electronics. The system was successfully operated for over thirty years, but eventually it proved difficult to maintain and its power output weakened so that it was switched off in 1998.

At the turn of the century it was decided to carry out a major refurbishment of the Royal Festival Hall, and the brief for the acoustics was to increase the reverberation time by passive means, rather than updating the electronic system. This meant some major alterations to the fabric of the hall, with a

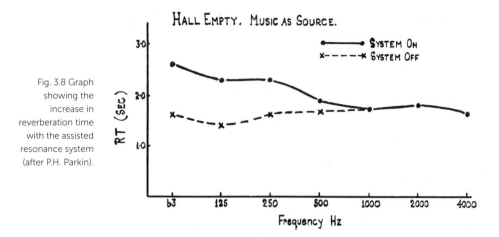

HALL EMPTY. MUSIC AS SOURCE.

●———● SYSTEM ON
×– – –× SYSTEM OFF

RT (SEC)

3·0

2·0

1·0

b3   125   250   500   1000   2000   4000

Frequency Hz

Fig. 3.8 Graph showing the increase in reverberation time with the assisted resonance system (after P.H. Parkin).

particular emphasis on increasing the weight of the ceiling and the wall linings to decrease the bass absorption. Part of this work involved removing the timber canopies above the stage and replacing them with special fabric canopies, which have the property of transmitting low-frequency sound but reflecting mid- and high-frequency sound. The intention was to enable the low-frequency sound

to reverberate around the whole hall, including the volume above the canopies, whilst providing mid-/high-frequency reflections to the orchestral players on stage.

Alterations were also made to the geometry of the stage to provide a better sequence of reflections to the musicians. A view towards the stage after the refurbishment is shown in Fig. 3.9.

Fig. 3.9 The Royal Festival Hall after the 2007 refurbishment, showing the fabric orchestral reflectors. (Courtesy Allies and Morrison Architects)

When the hall reopened in 2007, the acoustics were perceived to be improved although after a period of time it became evident that the hall had retained its reputation for clarity of sound but had not significantly improved its sense of reverberance or warmth. In particular, orchestral players still felt difficulty in hearing themselves and each other and they perceived a weakness in the bass sound.

The development of the acoustics of the Royal Festival Hall over a seventy-year period is a particularly interesting one. The design, which started in the late 1940s and continued in the early 1950s, embodied all the knowledge that was then available on concert-hall design, but the challenges of providing good acoustics for such a large audience were perhaps not fully appreciated, and the error in the ceiling construction was unfortunate. However, it stimulated the design of a pioneering electronic enhancement system that improved the acoustics for several decades. Unfortunately, attempts to implement remedial acoustic measures without resorting to electronics had a limited success.

The New York Philharmonic Hall (now The David Geffen Hall)

In the mid-1950s, the Metropolitan Opera Association in New York decided it needed a new opera house, and it was joined in its quest by the New York Philharmonic, who learned that their lease on Carnegie Hall would end in 1958. A site was identified at Lincoln Square, and an organization was formed called the Lincoln Center for the Performing Arts: this hall would accommodate the opera, the orchestra and the Juilliard School of Music.

The acoustician chosen for the design of the concert hall was Leo Beranek, the head of the acoustic consultancy Bolt, Beranek and Newman (BBN). Beranek had recently completed the successful renovation of the Tanglewood Music Shed in Lenox, Massachusetts (now known as the Koussevitzky Music Shed), which is a large outdoor venue for concerts. In anticipation of the Philharmonic Hall project, Beranek embarked on a comprehensive study of concert halls and opera houses around the world, fifty-four in total, which he published in a seminal book entitled *Music, Acoustics and Architecture*. The date of publication coincided with the opening of the hall in 1962 (Beranek 1962).

Based on his studies, Beranek decided that the most important requirement in a concert hall is acoustic intimacy. He went on to propose that this is obtained by reflecting surfaces close to the audience, and furthermore that the delay of the first reflection from these surfaces should be within 20ms – he called this criterion the initial time-delay gap. As well as this criterion, Beranek considered that the following qualities were also important in acoustical design: liveness, warmth, loudness, diffusion, ensemble, hall uniformity, freedom from echo and low background noise.

Beranek's initial design for the hall, which he handed to architect Max Abramovitz, was a shoebox with a volume of 24,000m³ (31,390yd³), and three shallow horizontal balconies stepping down towards the floor. The design also included diffusing elements on the walls. An array of acoustic reflectors were suspended over the first few rows of seats to direct early reflections to the audience. Beranek suggested that the design and layout of the seating should be compact if a capacity of 2,750 were to be reached, as at the Carnegie Hall; he advised that the generous seating proposed by the building committee would limit the capacity to 2,400.

The proposed plans were strongly criticized for having fewer seats than Carnegie, and under pressure, the architect proposed new plans. These involved changes to the hall itself, as the foundations of the outer walls had already been built. The architect managed to fit an additional 258 seats into the hall by bulging out the side walls. He also changed the design of the balconies by sweeping them down towards the stage, instead of stepping them down as recommended by Beranek. A comparison of Beranek's plan form before and after the architect's changes is shown in Fig. 3.10.

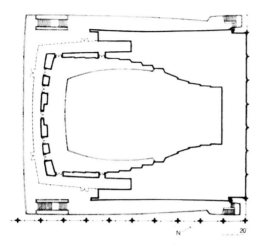

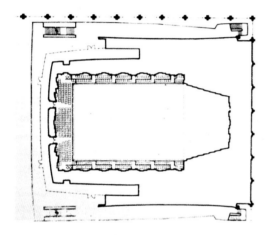

Fig. 3.10 New York Philharmonic Hall: comparison of Beranek's plan (below) with the amended plan by the architect Max Abramovitz.

Fig. 3.11 Ceiling reflectors in the New York Philharmonic Hall.

In an attempt to make these changes work acoustically, Beranek added more ceiling reflectors over most of the audience, and reiterated the need for diffusers on the walls. Unfortunately, owing to budget limitations, the diffusers were omitted and the ceiling panels were not motorized as required, which made acoustical adjustments almost impossible. Final tuning was carried out by Beranek during a series of test rehearsals with the New York Philharmonic Orchestra, and resulted, amongst other things, in the addition of more ceiling reflectors as shown in Fig. 3.11.

Soon after the opening concert in September 1962, criticisms of the acoustics began to appear in the press; the most damning was by the music critic of *The New York Times*, Harold Schonberg. He wrote:

> Philharmonic hall will never have the mellowness of the great ones of the past; the sound at best is going to be on the dry side, with clarity the primary consideration.

As the Philharmonic's regular season progressed, the criticisms in the press continued, with comments about the lack of bass sound, and that musicians were apprehensive about playing in the hall. Beranek responded to these criticisms by advising that the array of ceiling panels needed to lie on a plane as he had originally recommended in order to provide a greater surface area for reflecting bass frequencies; the individual panels themselves were too small to reflect the longer wavelengths. He also suggested that more diffusion was required to provide a more uniform coverage over the audience area.

However, the board of the Philharmonic decided to replace Beranek by new acoustic consultants. These consultants removed the ceiling reflectors together with some other changes – but the acoustic criticisms remained unabated. Eventually the board appointed a new acoustician, Cyril Harris, to work with a new architect, Philip Johnson, with a brief to gut the hall whilst leaving the building's original shell, and to build a new concert hall in its place. The work was supported by a wealthy donor, Avery Fisher, and the new hall was named after him.

What was remarkable about Harris' design is that it was very similar to Beranek's original design – namely a shoebox shape fitted with 2,742 seats of more compact design, together with stepped rather than sloping balconies. It was possible to remove the ceiling reflectors as the parallel side walls were now providing early lateral reflections.

The Avery Fisher Hall opened to the public in October 1976, and the concert goers, the musicians and the press were all complimentary. The critic Schonberg wrote 'a concert hall that New York will be proud of.'

In 1992 some alterations were made in the stage area by the acoustician, Russell Johnson, to improve the acoustics for musicians. These involved adding two adjustable reflectors above the stage, and diffusers on the stage walls. There alterations are shown in Fig. 3.12.

Despite all these changes, the acoustics of the hall were still not considered to be good enough, and in 2004 the orchestra announced that work would be undertaken that would focus on improving the hall's acoustics. In 2014, it was decided that Fisher's name would be removed and naming rights would be sold to the highest bidder to raise money for the refurbishment. David Geffen donated $100 million, and the hall is now named after him. However, in 2017 it was announced that the existing renovation plans for the hall had been scrapped.

The ongoing history of the Philharmonic Hall is one of the biggest and costliest acoustical disasters in the last seventy years. Beranek claims that contributors to this disaster were lack of time, money

Fig. 3.12 Acoustic reflectors and diffusers added to the stage of the Avery Fisher Hall.

and communication. The rumours and superstitions about the acoustics generated by the press were also particularly unhelpful. It is likely that Beranek's original design would have been at least reasonably successful, and that his attempts to adjust the altered design were hampered by the limited acoustical knowledge that was then available, as well as by the time and money constraints. There is also a balance to be struck between acoustical design, architecture, the client's aspirations, the critics and the response of the public. With such a high-profile building in such a high-profile location, getting all these factors to align is challenging.

The Berlin Philharmonie

In Europe, a few years after the completion of the Royal Festival Hall, work started on the design of a new concert hall for Berlin with around 2,400 seats. The architect was Hans Scharoun, and his vision, which was revolutionary, was to place the orchestra and conductor in the centre of the auditorium and surround them with audience. His concept of the space was that of a valley with the orchestra at the bottom surrounded by slopes of vineyard terraces.

He also intended that the distribution of the audience should be as egalitarian as possible, and split up the terraces into blocks, each containing between 100 and 300 audience members.

The blocks have surrounding walls, and this has the advantage of introducing many sound-reflecting surfaces in amongst the body of the audience. These surfaces provide useful early reflections, and when angled downwards they direct sound to adjacent blocks. A further advantage of these blocks is that they provide many more front-row balcony seats, which receive a strong, unimpeded direct sound. Furthermore, the rear walls of these blocks direct sound to the seats in front of them, particularly if tilted downwards, and compensate to some extent the loss of sound energy as sound grazes over the audience. A visual advantage of these audience blocks is that audience members in a block that is distant from the stage are less aware of the audience in front and below them, and so feel more intimately involved with the performance. A plan and section of the hall are shown in Fig. 3.13.

Scharoun was fortunate in having a first-class acoustician working with him, Lothar Cremer, who was somewhat sceptical about the acoustical success of an auditorium 'in the round'. However, Scharoun

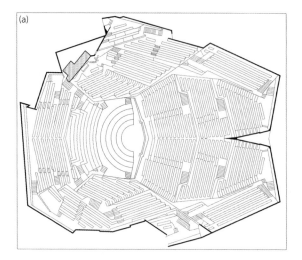

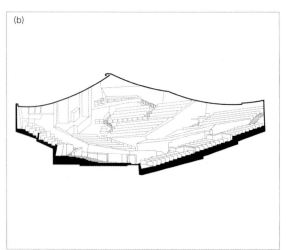

Fig. 3.13 Berlin Philharmonie: (a) plan and (b) section.

offered to accommodate Cremer's advice in every possible way if he was allowed to retain his original concept. A good example of this collaboration is that Scharoun quite naturally intended to place a dome over the auditorium, whereas Cremer pointed out that this would cause serious focusing of sound. Cremer suggested that a convex shape for the ceiling would be far better and would provide a nearly equal distribution of sound over the audience.

Scharoun accepted this advice and designed a tent-like structure comprising convex surfaces. Where the two main convex surfaces meet high up above the stage, a type of cavity is formed which is acoustically undesirable, and it is here that large reflectors, called 'sails', were suspended to reflect sound downwards towards the stage. These were very much considered by Scharoun as architectural elements.

Another advantage of the tent-like geometry is that it creates a low ceiling above the rear seats around the perimeter of the hall, so these seats receive strong reflections, which enhance the sound quality in these locations.

Although Sharoun may have wanted a completely in-the-round arrangement with equal seating on all sides, this was not considered feasible with the traditional layout of an orchestra, so there is a frontal bias to the seating distribution with only 10 per cent of the seats being behind the orchestra. This suits a majority of listeners who prefer to sit in front of the orchestra to be able to hear the correct balance. Others prefer to be closer to the performers and enjoy sitting at the sides or behind. A view of the auditorium is shown in Fig. 3.14.

For those members of the audience sitting at the sides or behind, the balance of the sound is affected by the directionality of the instruments and the shadowing produced by the player's bodies. The voices of singers are particularly directional, and are somewhat weaker for the audience sitting behind them.

Fig. 3.14 Berlin Philharmonie. (Photo: Peter Adamik)

The acoustics of the Berlin Philharmonie have developed a very high reputation, which has been maintained for many years. The sound is considered to have high clarity with ample reverberance, with the best balance occurring in the seats in front of the stage. The balance is less good for the seats to the side and behind the stage, but this is preferred by some listeners. What is remarkable about the design is that it has spawned many similar designs, which have become known as the 'vineyard terrace' halls – their popularity has continued into the twenty-first century.

The Sydney Opera House

The Sydney Opera House, the design of which began in 1957, presented a challenge to the acoustic consultant, the Danish acoustician Vilhelm Lassen Jordan, because both orchestral concerts and opera were to be accommodated in the building. This led initially to the design of a multipurpose hall with variable acoustic elements that would enable the auditorium to be adjusted to suit each type of performance. However, this concept was later abandoned, and the main auditorium was designed purely as a concert hall.

This in itself was challenging, as the concert hall had to be fitted within the external shells that define the iconic appearance of the building. A further challenge was to provide a seating capacity of 2,800, which is very large if acoustic uniformity is to be achieved.

Jordan originally opted for a plan shape that adopted the acoustical qualities of the 'shoebox' form, as he believed this was the best approach for providing good acoustics (Jordan 1973). However, the architect, Utzon, was keen to design something more adventurous, and later brought in a second acoustician, Professor Lothar Cremer from Germany, to provide a second opinion.

Disagreements about all aspects of the design during this period were numerous, and Utzon eventually resigned; he was replaced by the local architect Peter Hall. This led to a redesign of the main hall, which was now solely a concert hall: its form became

Fig. 3.15 Concert hall in Sydney Opera House (prior to the 2020 refurbishment).

an elongated hexagon on plan, with the stage located towards the centre and choir seating behind. The ceiling above the stage is particularly high at 25m (82ft), and orchestral reflectors in the form of circular rings were suspended above the stage. A view of the concert hall is shown in Fig. 3.15.

The reverberation time in the hall is close to the ideal value of 2 seconds and has a flat frequency response. However, the acoustic reputation developed in the years after opening (1973) was not always favourable, with the orchestral players being particularly concerned about not being able to hear each other well; the violinists felt they had to emphasize their bowing so much that they nicknamed this technique the 'Sydney scrape'! This led to a number of exercises to make improvements.

The latest of these, and the most comprehensive, was carried out in the years 2019 to 2022, and involves principally a new stage layout, the replacement of the orchestral 'ring' reflectors with much larger panels, together with additional reflecting panels throughout the auditorium. The improvements to the acoustics during early test performances were highly appreciated by both orchestral players and listeners.

New Research in Auditorium Acoustics

From the 1950s onwards, researchers began to investigate other factors, besides reverberation time, to account for variations in acoustic quality between different seating areas. It emerged that reflections arriving at a listener soon after the direct sound (within 80ms) are integrated by the brain together with the direct sound, reinforcing it, and therefore increasing the clarity of sound in a room. This implied that clarity and its balance with reverberance can be controlled by the number and strength of early reflections.

Towards the end of the 1960s, the acoustician, Harold Marshall, proposed that early reflections that arrive at a listener from a lateral direction give rise to an increased sense of 'spaciousness' when listening to orchestral music (Marshall 1967). His hypothesis was confirmed by the experimentation of Michael Barron, who termed the effect 'spatial impression', and showed that the relevant time period for these reflections was also within 80ms of the direct sound. In detail, this effect is perceived as a broadening of the sound source, which can extend to complete 'envelopment' by the musical sound (Barron 1971).

This highly significant acoustical development was first applied by Harold Marshall in the design of a new concert hall in New Zealand: Christchurch Town Hall, completed in 1972.

Christchurch Town Hall, New Zealand

The architects for Christchurch Town Hall, Warren and Mahoney, proposed a faceted, elliptical plan shape with a balcony cantilevered from each of the facets. In effect, each of the facets has associated with it two seating blocks, one at stalls level and one at balcony level. The main stalls are on a flat floor, which was a requirement of the brief. The capacity of the hall

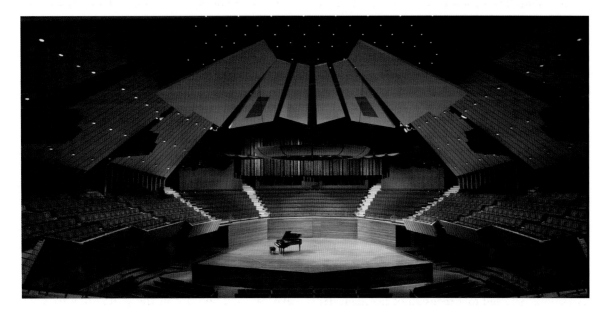

Fig. 3.16 Christchurch Town Hall, New Zealand. (Courtesy Marshall Day Acoustics)

is around 2,500, and owing to the elliptical shape, no seat is further than 28m (92ft) from the stage front.

The fundamental aim of the acoustical design was to direct ample early lateral reflections to the seating in support of Marshall's theory that such reflections give a sense of 'spaciousness'. Marshall was not particularly concerned with the overall shape of this hall, but rather, with surfaces within the hall that direct sound towards the audience. He referred to this type of hall as a 'directed reflection sequence hall'.

One of the most striking features of the hall is the array of large acoustic reflectors around the hall, one above each seating block, with some additional ones above the stage area. Each of these reflectors provides lateral reflections into the adjacent balcony seating block, and into the stalls. At the rear, opposite the stage, the reflectors are made of two contiguous panels at an angle, like the back of an open book, to direct reflections to either side.

Additional reflections to the stalls are provided by angled balcony fronts. A further feature is the inclination of the balcony soffits, which augment reflections to seats overhung by the balcony. Reflections to support musicians on stage are provided by overhead surfaces. A view of the hall is shown in Fig. 3.16.

An elliptical plan shape carries the risk of focusing; this is largely avoided by the shadowing caused by the large acoustic reflectors, and at stalls level, by the inclined balcony soffit and seating rake. Small areas that remained exposed were treated with sound-absorbent material.

The volume of the hall is large, at 20,700m³ (27,075yd³), and generates a reverberation time of over 2 seconds when occupied. Subjectively, the outstanding feature is the high degree of clarity in the sound, which is balanced by the long reverberation; interestingly, the sense of 'spaciousness' is adequate but not particularly pronounced.

Unfortunately the hall was badly damaged during the earthquake of 2011, but with the help of the original acoustic consultants, Marshall Day, it was rebuilt and re-opened in 2019 with the aim of retaining the original acoustic response.

Barbican Concert Hall, London

The Barbican concert hall was designed in the 1960s and 1970s, and presented a great opportunity for London to have a world class 2,000-seat venue. Unfortunately, the balance between architecture and acoustics tipped too far in favour of the architecture, and the result has not been a success in terms of acoustic quality. The plan shape does not follow the classical shoebox form, but rather the opposite, where the width is greater than the length. A plan and section of the hall is shown in Fig. 3.17.

Another departure from the classical style is the profiling of the ceiling, which is criss-crossed by very deep beams with a depth of 3.7m (12ft). The necessity for these was to support a heavy roof, on top of

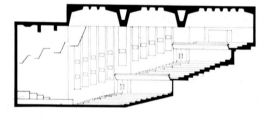

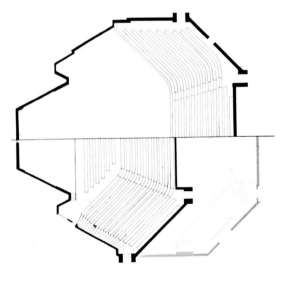

Fig. 3.17 Plan and section of the Barbican hall.

which there was a plan for a sculpture court. These deep beams cause a shadowing of sound across the ceiling, and hence result in an uneven distribution over the seating. Furthermore, the deep recesses or bays created by these beams could cause undesirable localized acoustic effects to occur. To eliminate these potential problems, the recesses were filled with 2,000 glass spheres of three different sizes, the largest being 800mm in diameter and the smallest 325mm, as shown in Fig. 3.18. Model tests at 1:8-scale showed that these spheres were beneficial for providing lateral sound, which was clearly lacking in such a wide hall.

However, on completion of the hall in the early 1980s, measurements of reverberation time gave a result of 1.6 seconds at mid frequencies, with a similarly low value in the bass; these values were considerably lower than intended. An early remedial measure was to remove a bay of the glass spheres; this produced a modest increase in reverberation time, but the removal of more spheres had little further effect. Measurements of the sound absorption of the seating gave values that were higher than expected, and modifications were made to reduce this – although again, this did not have much of an effect.

Following the official opening of the hall in 1982, no further significant remedial measures were implemented at that time, although the acoustic quality remained a concern. A view of the hall is shown in Fig. 3.19. Ten years later, a number of phases of remedial measures were implemented – the most dramatic of these, completed in 2001, was the suspension of acoustic reflectors in the ceiling zone. These improved the clarity of the sound, but at the expense of a shorter reverberation time. The acoustic quality after these remedial measures was considered to be improved, but still not of a world class standard.

When Sir Simon Rattle agreed to become the principal conductor of the London Symphony Orchestra in 2017, whose home is in the Barbican hall, plans began for a new concert hall in London. At the time of writing, these plans are still at a very early stage.

Fig. 3.18 Suspended spheres in the ceiling of the Barbican hall.

Fig. 3.19 The Barbican concert hall.

Segerstrom Hall, California

Segerstrom Hall, named after its major benefactor, is a 3,000-seat, multipurpose auditorium within the Segerstrom Center for the Arts in California. It was formally opened in September 1986, and caters for performances of orchestral music, opera, musicals, ballet and drama.

The architect was Charles Lawrence, who, together with theatre consultant John von Szeliski, formed a design team with the acoustical consultants Harold Marshall, Jerald Hyde and Dennis Paoletti. A remarkable aspect of this collaboration is that the acoustical requirements were the dominant factor in defining the geometry of the auditorium.

The acoustic brief was principally to provide listening conditions for various types of music that would have a high degree of clarity coupled with ample reverberance and a sense of spaciousness or envelopment. To satisfy these requirements the design made considerable use of the pioneering work of Marshall regarding the subjective impression of sound in auditoria.

The requirements for the auditorium were for a large, multipurpose space with at least 3,000 seats. They were all to be on one side of a proscenium stage. These requirements forced the initial plan shape of the auditorium into a fan. This ensures that all the seats have good sightlines and are as close to the stage as possible. As the rearmost seats were not to be further than 43m from the stage – a criterion for musical and operatic presentations – balconies had to be incorporated. However, the arrangement of 3,000 seats in a fan-shaped space resulted in a width at the rear of 50m (164ft). The acoustical implications of this are serious, particularly for the seats near the centre, which are a long way from sidewall boundaries. The ceiling is also distant because a large ceiling height was necessary to achieve adequate reverberation.

For the centre third of the seats, the delay of the first early reflections occurs in the range 60 to 95ms, whereas they should preferably be within 80ms. This means that without corrective measures, the balance between early and late sound would be biased too far towards late sound for symphonic music.

To reduce the delay of early reflections and to increase their level, the seating was subdivided into four tiers, which provide extra vertical surfaces in the centre of the fan, as shown in the plan in Fig. 3.20.

These extra surfaces act as 'sidewalls', and in each case are appropriately angled to direct early lateral reflections to the seating tier below. Thus the seats near the centre of the overall fan are aurally in a narrower room of 20 to 25m (65 to 82ft), where the spatial impression is enhanced. Early lateral reflections are also provided by the sidewalls of the fan,

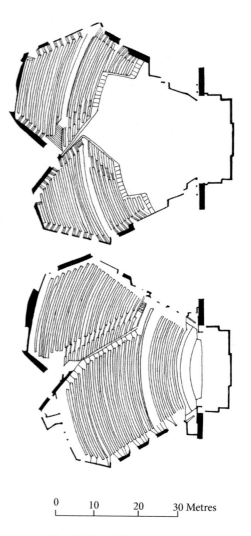

0   10   20   30 Metres

Fig. 3.20 Plan of Segerstrom Hall.

which are subdivided into steps and appropriately angled. A view showing the subdivided seating can be seen in Fig. 3.21.

Additional early reflections arrive from the large reflectors suspended within the volume of the auditorium, as shown in Fig. 3.22; these reflections have a time delay in the range 20 to 80ms. By appropriate angling of the reflectors, many of the reflections arrive from lateral directions.

Those reflectors nearest the stage are made diffusing according to a mathematical profile developed by Professor Manfred Schroeder (1975), so that lateral

Fig. 3.21 The seating tiers at Segerstrom Hall. (Courtesy Jerry Hyde)

Fig. 3.22 Reflections from overhead reflectors at Segerstrom Hall (after Marshall, Day and Hyde).

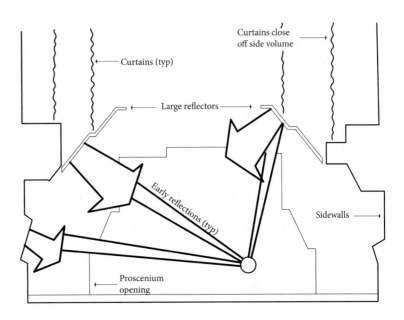

Fig. 3.23
Segerstrom Hall:
side view of the
auditorium.

reflections from these surfaces are diffuse and avoid the possibility of strong specular reflections that could cause image shift. These diffusing reflectors, which look like grooved surfaces, can be seen adjacent to the stage in Fig. 3.23.

An additional feature that provides variability in the acoustics is the use of banners, which can be extended or retracted. They are located beyond the main reflectors from the listeners' viewpoint, so they do not interfere with the early reflection sequence. With the banners extended, the 'early' sound remains essentially the same, whereas the late sound is reduced, thus providing higher clarity suitable for opera and speech.

The complete design was comprehensively tested in a 1:10-scale acoustic model, and the results provided reassurance that the design parameters would be met. When the hall was completed, the same range of tests was carried out at full scale, with impressive results. The mean values for all the acoustic parameters were favourable, which was a notable achievement for an audience of 3,000. The reverberation time is long – 2.4 seconds when unoccupied, and 2 seconds when occupied – and the clarity index is high for the length of reverberation time. This can be expected in a directed reflection sequence hall, where ample early reflections are provided. Particularly notable are the high degree of early lateral energy and the high level of loudness – a great accomplishment in such a large space.

Subjective tests were also carried out with various musical ensembles, with the conclusion that the sound was characterized as having a high level of clarity, reverberance and loudness, together with a great sense of intimacy and envelopment. There was also a remarkable consistency of response between the listeners and also between the seats. When questioned, the musicians uniformly commented on the fact that they were able to hear each other, as well as receiving good support from the hall.

In summary, the design of Segerstrom Hall was dominated by the acoustical requirements. These were challenging because of the size of the audience and the requirements for multipurpose use. The solution to the problem was ingenious, not only by making every bounding surface an important acoustic reflector, but also by forming additional reflecting surfaces within the body of the seating, and by suspending reflectors from the ceiling. This was a bold design approach to a demanding acoustical brief, and it is gratifying that the outcome was successful.

Birmingham Symphony Hall

The form of the 2,200-seat Birmingham Symphony Hall, which opened in 1991, was defined by the acoustician Russell Johnson of Artec Consultants in New York, whose design directions were implemented by the architects Percy Thomas Partnership. Russell Johnson was one of the first acousticians to demand that the acoustical design of a concert hall should come first, and should then be followed by the architectural design; this was a bold and challenging approach, but he was successful at it. He was not influenced by the trend in 'vineyard terrace' design, but reverted back to the nineteenth-century designs

of a parallel-sided hall with a horizontal ceiling. The only significant departure from the classical shape was the reverse splay of the walls in plan towards the rear of the hall, which is a useful feature for providing early lateral reflections.

The dimensions of the hall follow the classical double-cube proportions of nineteenth-century halls, although adjusted for a larger capacity and more generous seating; the width is 27m (88.5ft), the height 23m (75ft) and the length 57m (187ft).

A unique feature of this hall, which differentiates it from nineteenth-century halls, is the so-called reverberation chamber, which can be coupled to the hall to increase the reverberation. This concept was first implemented in the hall's older sibling, the Eugene McDermott Hall in Dallas, which was completed in 1989. Fig. 3.24 shows a 3D diagram of this hall, where the volume of the reverberation chamber (shown in green) can be seen to be almost one third of the volume of the concert hall.

In the Birmingham Hall, the reverberation chamber is located at the stage end; it is U-shaped,

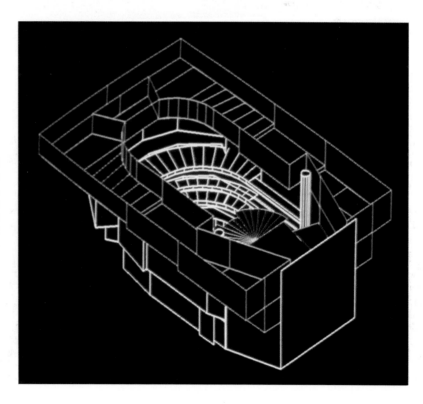

Fig. 3.24 3D diagram of Eugene McDermott Hall, showing the reverberation chamber (in green).

and extends from floor level to above the ceiling. It has a volume of 10,300m³ (13,470yd³), which is close to half of the volume of the auditorium, which is 25,000m³ (32,700yd³). The reverberation chamber can be coupled to the auditorium via massive doors, which can be opened to different extents to control the degree of coupling.

The purpose of the reverberation chamber is to increase the reverberance in the auditorium by allowing the reverberant sound in the chamber to enhance the reverberation in the auditorium. This feature is intended to provide optimal conditions for orchestral or choral works, which require a long reverberation time. When the hall was completed and used in configurations where the chamber doors were either opened or closed, audiences were generally unable to hear the difference, and this subjective perception was supported by objective measurements of reverberation time, which showed only small differences (Barron 2010). The concept of the reverberation chamber for varying the acoustics was not fully realized in this project, but was developed more successfully in future halls, for example at Lucerne.

Another feature of the hall that enables adjustment of the acoustics is the stage canopy; this is a heavy device weighing 42 tonnes, which is adjustable in height. The aim of the canopy is to provide reflections to the musicians on stage and to the audience in the front stalls. Typical heights above stage level range from 10m (33ft) for small ensembles, to 14m (46ft) for a full orchestra. The heavy weight ensures that low frequencies are reflected as well as higher frequencies. A view of the concert hall is shown in Fig. 3.25.

When the hall is used for amplified music or speech, movable sound-absorbing panels can be

Fig. 3.25 Birmingham Symphony Hall.

deployed on the sides and rear of the auditorium; they have a total area of 625m³ (818yd³).

Another key feature of the hall is the very low background noise level in the hall: effectively it is inaudible. This required a very carefully designed ventilation system, and structural isolation from a nearby busy main-line railway. The advantage of such a low background noise level is that it permits a greater dynamic range for the sound, so that, for example, pianissimos can be heard distinctly.

The overall design of this hall includes the desirable elements of the successful nineteenth-century halls, together with the added facilities of varying the acoustics. In the third decade after its opening, the acoustics of the hall remain highly regarded by most listeners, and the eminent acoustician Leo Beranek has rated it as one of the ten best concert halls in the world (Beranek 2016). By contrast, Barron has observed that a number of acousticians in the UK have rated the hall only as 'good', and that the sound in the rear stalls is favoured to that in the top tier – a possible reason is a concentration of early lateral reflections and early reflections in the stalls, which provide an enveloping and loud sound in that seating area.

In summary, the acoustics of the hall are undoubtedly considered a success by most, and the adoption of the nineteenth-century shoebox shape in the twentieth century was a good approach. A criticism is the commitment of Artec consultants to incorporating a reverberation chamber: this was a costly element of the design and did not fulfil its promise.

Bridgewater Hall, Manchester

The design of the 2,400-seat Bridgewater Hall followed closely on the heels of the Birmingham hall; the architects were RHWL, with acoustic consultancy by Arup. The concept of the acoustic design was to keep the hall narrow to ensure strong lateral reflections, but to include some terracing, as in the 'vineyard terrace' halls, to provide additional surfaces

Fig. 3.26 1:50-scale model of Bridgewater Hall.

for early reflections. In effect, the acoustic design of the hall combined the attributes of the shoebox halls with those of the 'vineyard terrace' halls.

Extensive tests were carried out on the design using a 1:50-scale acoustic model, shown in Fig. 3.26, which enabled many details to be optimized. For example, the design of the ceiling profile initially comprised a series of regular ascending steps like the underside of a staircase. Acoustic modelling showed that consecutive reflections from these steps had equal time delays, which interfered with each other, causing an undesirable tonal coloration of sound; this effect is sometimes referred to as a 'picket-fence' echo. This was avoided by alternately angling each step so that the reflections were directed into different paths – in effect the reflections were diffused. This can be seen in a view of the hall shown in Fig. 3.27.

The background noise in the auditorium is extremely low so as not to cause any distraction from external noise sources. This was achieved by completely isolating the envelope of the auditorium from adjacent spaces by supporting it on steel springs. The ventilation system is also extremely quiet, with very slow-moving air permeating from under the seats.

Considerable attention was paid to checking the sound absorption of all the elements and surfaces in the auditorium, particularly the seating. The latter was specified in detail in terms of sound absorption, and was subsequently measured in a reverberation chamber to check compliance.

Fig. 3.27
Bridgewater
Hall: view of the
stage and ceiling.
(Courtesy Arup)

The meticulous attention to the acoustic design using models, and the attention to the absorption of the internal materials, was reflected in the measurement results when the hall was completed. The mid-frequency reverberation time was exactly 2 seconds when occupied, with a rise in the bass as intended. The other parameters, such as clarity index and early lateral energy fraction, all have textbook values. A view of the concert hall is shown in Fig. 3.28.

The hall was officially opened in 1996, and has become highly regarded for its acoustic quality, although with some minor quibbles by critical listeners. It has not outranked the great halls in the world, although it is possible that it could have done so with a little more sound diffusion on the main reflecting surfaces.

Contemporary Opera House Design

Opera house designs during this period have generally been very conservative, and many have adhered to the traditional horseshoe plan shape of the eighteenth century. Examples of such opera houses are Glyndebourne Opera House in the UK, the Operaen in Copenhagen, and Den Norske Opera in Oslo. However, a number of opera houses have diverged from the traditional form, such as the Guangzhou Opera house in China.

Glyndebourne Opera House, England

The original Glyndebourne Opera House, situated on a country estate near Lewes, was built in 1934, but by the 1980s the opera company had outgrown

Fig. 3.28 Bridgewater Hall: view of the auditorium. (Courtesy Arup)

its building. The new opera house was in fact the first opera house to be built in England since the previous Glyndebourne, which shows how infrequently such venues are built. The design of the new Glyndebourne Opera House, by architects Hopkins Architects, working with theatre consultants Theatre Projects, was a traditional horseshoe plan shape, and was initially surmounted by a dome.

This presented the acoustical design team at Arup with considerable challenges relating to the focusing of sound by the curved drum of the auditorium, the curved balcony fronts, and the domed ceiling. The focusing by the curved drum, which was constructed of brickwork, was countered by locating convex panels made of timber on the exposed parts of the drum that were not obscured by seating.

The shape of the ceiling, which was raised in the centre, was developed to comprise mainly flat surfaces, rather than curves, in order to reduce focusing; where circular geometry remained it was made heavily diffusing. The balcony fronts were designed not only to reduce focusing, but to direct early reflections and early lateral reflections towards the audience. This involved geometrical gymnastics, as the balconies at different levels required different orientations to send the reflections in the appropriate directions. A plan and section of the opera house are shown in Fig. 3.29.

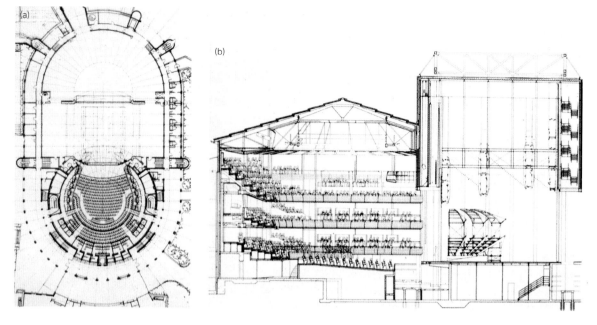

Fig. 3.29 Plan and section of Glyndebourne Opera House.

The seating was considered particularly important in terms of its acoustic absorption, and it was specially designed for the project and tested before installation; a bird's eye view of the seating layout is shown in Fig. 3.30.

The completed Glyndebourne Opera House opened in 1994 and has developed a very high reputation for its acoustics after nearly three decades of performances. A view of the auditorium is shown in Fig. 3.31.

Fig. 3.30 Glyndebourne Opera House: a bird's eye view of the seating. (Courtesy Arup)

Fig. 3.31 Glyndebourne Opera House. (Courtesy Arup)

Grange Park Opera House, England

Twenty years after the completion of Glyndebourne Opera House, a new opera house was being planned on another country estate, this time near Guildford, 35 miles from London. The estate is West Horsley Place, and the opera company is Grange Park Opera. The client was in no doubt that it should have a traditional horseshoe form based on the Teatro alla Scala in Milan, although somewhat smaller, with 700 seats. The architects were Tim Ronalds Architects, with acoustic consultancy by Ramboll. The plan and section are shown in Fig. 3.32.

Fig. 3.32 Grange Park Opera House: plan and section. (Architects: Tim Ronalds Architects)

Fig. 3.33 Grange Park Opera House.

Owing to a limited budget for the project, the construction materials were very simple, comprising mainly masonry, concrete and heavy timber; the heavy timber was specified to avoid excessive sound absorption at bass frequencies. The horseshoe plan shape inevitably causes some focusing, but because of the small size of the auditorium the delay of the reflections is limited, and the focusing moderately enhances the loudness of singers' voices in the rear stalls; this of course is beneficial in balancing the singers and orchestra.

Grange Park Opera opened for its first season in its new house in 2017, and the reports in the press about the acoustics were exceptionally complimentary. It seems that the traditional opera house form recreated in the twenty-first century, particularly at small scale, can be very successful. A view of the auditorium is shown in Fig. 3.33.

Guangzhou Opera House, China

The Guangzhou Opera House in China is a twenty-first-century opera house seating 1,800, which has departed from the classical design. It was designed by Zaha Hadid Architects with acoustic consultancy by Marshall Day Acoustics. Zaha Hadid had previously submitted a design for the Cardiff Bay Opera House in Wales, which had an asymmetrical plan, and although it won first prize in the competition there was considerable resistance to the innovative design and the project was not funded. This was a sad loss to the Welsh operatic community, which has a great tradition in operatic and choral singing. However, the essence of that design, particularly in terms of asymmetry, was adopted for the Guangzhou project.

The acoustical aim was to provide high clarity but at the same time ample reverberance, as the venue was to be used for orchestral concerts as well as opera. To achieve this, it was necessary to adjust the angles of walls and other surfaces to direct early reflections to the audience. It was also necessary to make certain surfaces diffusing in order to avoid late reflections, which would be detrimental.

The opera house, shown in Fig. 3.34, was opened in 2011 and was well received in the press. Jonathan Glancy wrote in *The Guardian* newspaper 'The auditorium proves to be a further wonder, a great grotto like a shark's mouth set under a constellation of fairy lights.' He then quotes Sir Harold Marshall who said

Fig. 3.34
Guangzhou Opera
House. (Courtesy
Marshall Day
Acoustics)

'there are very few asymmetrical auditoriums. But asymmetry can be used to play with sound in very satisfying ways; it's more of a challenge.'

The design of Guangzhou Opera House is clearly a departure from the traditional form, but it remains to be seen whether this kind of departure will be sustained or whether the traditional form will prevail.

The Elisabeth Murdoch Hall, Melbourne

The Elisabeth Murdoch Hall was designed by Australian architects Ashton, Raggatt McDougall with acoustic consultancy by Arup; it was built in 2008 and is a reversion to the shoebox form. It is an example where the client body, which included musical advisers, was convinced that the classical shoebox-shaped hall still produces the best acoustic quality. The brief therefore for this 1,000-seat space was a classic shoebox geometry, but interpreted architecturally in a contemporary style. The hall is, in effect, a recital hall, as the size of the stage is designed to accommodate a chamber orchestra of up to forty-five musicians. It also caters for other uses such as chamber opera, early music, jazz and contemporary music.

The shoebox geometry gave rise to a hall width of 20m (66ft), in order to provide strong lateral sound to the audience. The length was set at 37m (121ft), which permits an audience of 1,000 to be accommodated on two levels: the stalls and the balcony. The balcony at the rear wraps around the sidewalls of the hall, providing additional seating. The soffits of these side balconies, in combination with the sidewalls, provide early reflections to the stalls. The rake of the stalls is gently angled to give good sight-lines and soundlines. The ceiling height was set at 17m (56ft), which provides a volume per seat of 9m^3 (11.75yd^3), providing a reverberation time of around 2 seconds.

The contemporary aspect of the design is expressed by the strategy for diffusion. This aimed to provide limited high frequency diffusion on the walls at low level to maintain the strength of early and early lateral reflections. Higher up the walls the diffusion becomes a little more pronounced, and it is yet more pronounced on the ceiling.

The timber panels forming the walls and ceiling are heavy to preserve bass sound, and are stepped in and out to provide medium-scale diffusion. Whole sections of walls and ceiling are modulated to provide large-scale diffusion. In addition, the surface layer of the panels is grooved or cut away to form a random pattern, and this also provides some diffusion at high frequencies. Around the stage, the panels are smaller but also stepped, modulated and patterned to provide diffuse reflections back to the orchestra and some to the audience. A detail of the diffusing surfaces is shown in Fig. 3.35.

To provide the musicians on stage with sufficient early sound so that they can hear each other well and also hear themselves, an appropriate sequence of early reflections is required. The use of an orchestral reflector was not acceptable to the client (none generally exist in classical shoebox halls) and so early reflections for the orchestra are provided by articulating and shaping the surfaces around the stage. The strategy was to lower the ceiling above the stage in a series of steps, which created ledges around the stage enclosure to provide early 'cue-ball' reflections.

Acoustic modelling of the design was carried out using both an acoustic computer model and an acoustic scale model. The scale model shown in Fig. 3.36, which was constructed at 1:25 scale, was particularly useful in checking the acoustical effect of the diffusing surfaces, which were far too detailed for computer modelling.

Fig. 3.35 Details of diffusing surfaces, Elisabeth Murdoch Hall.

Fig. 3.36 Acoustic scale model of the Elisabeth Murdoch Hall.

Fig. 3.37 Elisabeth Murdoch Hall.

Variable absorption to accommodate other uses of the hall, such as amplified performances and jazz, is provided by individual acoustic banners which are deployed on the side walls and rear wall. Since it opened, the hall has gained a very high reputation for its acoustics and was voted by an independent survey as the best recital hall in Australia. A view of the hall is shown in Fig. 3.37.

Krakow Concert Hall in the Name of Krzysztof Penderecki, Poland

Although shoebox-shaped concert halls remained popular for smaller venues and with those clients who considered them to provide the best acoustics, the dominant fashion in the latter half of the twentieth century and the beginning of the twenty-first century was for 'vineyard terrace' or surround-type halls based on the Berlin Philharmonie. Key examples in the UK are St David's Hall in Cardiff and the Waterfront Hall in Belfast.

When it came to prepare a competition brief for a new 1,800-seat concert hall in Krakow located within a new congress centre, the requirement was, not surprisingly, for a form based on an amphitheatre layout. There was, however, a twist to the brief in that the stage was to be located at one end of the hall rather than centrally, to provide easy access. This concept has one significant advantage over a fully surround hall because the audience are all in front of the stage. This advantage will become more evident as recent surround halls are discussed, such as the Elbphilharmonie in Hamburg.

The competition was won in 2005 by the Krakovian architectural practice Ingarden and Ewy, who brought in the international architect Arata Izosaki to help specifically with the design of the auditorium; the acoustic consultancy was by Ramboll. The construction of the hall was strongly supported by the eminent composer Krzysztof Penderecki, a Krakow resident, and the hall was later named after him.

The fundamental geometry of the main auditorium bears a strong resemblance to the Berlin Philharmonie, albeit truncated at the stage end: the basic parameters are a volume per seat of 10m^3 (13yd^3), a maximum room height above the stalls floor of 18m (59ft), and a width at stalls level of 23m (75ft).

Fig. 3.38 The Krakow Concert Hall in the name of Krzysztof Penderecki. (Courtesy Ingarden and Ewy Architects)

The distance from the stage edge to the furthest seat for an orchestral concert configuration is 32m (105ft). A view of the auditorium during an orchestral concert is shown in Fig. 3.38.

To enable a change from concert to congress mode, approximately 800m² of acoustic absorption in the form of drop-down banners was incorporated, mainly along the side and rear walls. The banners can also be adjusted in banks to provide a range of reverberation times to suit various types of performance.

The design development involved optimizing configurations of the vineyard terraces and the inclinations of the terrace walls to provide an optimum sequence of early reflections incident on the seating. The acoustic performance was checked with an acoustic computer model, and also a physical model at 1:50 scale. The scale model provided valuable confirmation that the specified reverberation times with and without variable absorption would be achieved. Also, it confirmed the value of having an orchestral reflector above the stage, which was initially queried by the architect.

The acoustic proposal for the orchestral reflector was that it should comprise an array of panels approximately equivalent to half the area of the stage and that these should be variable in height but typically set at 8 to 10m (26 to 33ft) above the stage. This was interpreted by the architect as a collection of organic shapes of similar size, distributed fairly uniformly above the stage area.

In terms of surface finishes, the walls of the auditorium are lined with timber, which, as well as being aesthetically pleasing, is modelled to provide varying degrees of diffusion. At a lower level – namely, the stage enclosure and lower balcony walls – the diffusion is based on battens of different depths, similar to a Schroeder diffuser without fins, but also set at different angles in the vertical plane. At a higher level, on the upper balcony walls, the diffusion is larger scale and consists of a mix of convex geometries together with battens.

The acoustic characteristics of the upstage wall can be varied by means of an arrangement of movable and rotatable panels. These are diffusing on one side and sound absorbing on the other; they can also be retracted to provide a plane reflective upstage wall.

The ceiling is made up of multiple layers of plasterboard to provide sufficient weight to minimize low frequency absorption. It has a gentle convex shape when viewed from the audience plane, and provides moderate diffusion over the seating area. The orchestral reflectors are also made up of multiple layers of plasterboard. The floor is a heavy build-up of plywood and timber. The seats are designed, as usual, to limit the variation in room acoustics between the occupied and unoccupied condition.

The completed concert hall is now well established as an international orchestral venue and has the advantages of a surround hall but with the whole audience frontal to the stage. With its variable acoustics, it also functions well as a conference venue.

Paris Philharmonie

The design of a new concert hall for Paris was a very high-profile project, and the selection of the design team, which started in 2007, was very competitive. The French practice Atelier Jean Nouvel won the architectural commission; Nouvel had previously designed the concert hall in Lucerne, and also the one in Copenhagen. The acoustic design was won by Marshall Day Acoustics, with Harold Marshall leading the conceptual design. Nouvel had previously worked with the acoustician Yasuhisa Toyota of Nagata Acoustics on the Copenhagen Hall, and controversially, invited him to join the design team as a special adviser.

The acoustic brief was drafted by Kahle Acoustics, who specified a hall with 2,400 seats with acoustic quality comparable to the best recent halls, and with an innovative architectural concept. It also specified a central stage for classical music concerts, and a frontal stage for amplified concerts. Although the brief was careful to avoid showing any preference between a shoebox or vineyard shape, the requirement for a central stage indicated some type of 'surround' hall.

Harold Marshall, in developing the concept for the hall, recognized the similarity between the brief and his design of the Christchurch Town Hall. The key parallels were these: a new typology, surrounding seat layout, independent control of the early sound of the source and the later sound of the room, and clarity together with reverberance. This led Marshall to consider a 'room within a room' as a possible solution – he referred to this as a 'bicameral arrangement' (Marshall & Day 2015).

Marshall's initial idea was to create an inner space whose surfaces provided early reflections and a large volume above for reverberation. This was later changed because there was a height restriction on the building, and the large volume was moved to the sides of the inner space. The winning design proposed two nested chambers: an inner space producing visual and acoustical intimacy between audience and performer, and an outer space with its own architectural and acoustical presence (Marshall & Day 2015); an early sketch by Harold Marshall is shown in Fig. 3.39.

In developing the concept, the demand for high clarity and envelopment meant that the surfaces defining the boundary between the two chambers became the primary acoustic reflectors in the hall. Also, there was no possibility of adjusting the opening

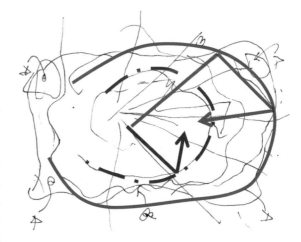

Fig. 3.39 Early sketch of acoustic concept by Harold Marshall. The inner volume (red) defines the early response, and the outer volume (blue) defines the late response. (Courtesy Marshall Day Acoustics)

between the inner and outer volume, so the design had to make sure that the degree of coupling between the inner and outer chambers was right.

The design involved a number of key elements, all of which had an influence on the acoustic outcome and needed to be developed thoroughly. The inner volume controls the distance between audience and stage; it also controls the distribution of the audience and its absorption, and hence the reverberation time and loudness. The outer volume controls the late response of the room. The opening between the two controls late energy returning into the inner volume. The suspended reflectors (called 'nuages') provide early lateral reflections, whilst the balcony fronts and walls (called 'ribbons') provide first- and second-order early lateral reflections. The canopy above the stage provides ensemble reflections to the musicians (Scelo *et al* 2015).

The shaping and articulation of the reflecting surfaces was optimized by extensive computer modelling, and was supported by scale modelling. Finalization of the design also involved making key surfaces diffusing to ensure an even distribution of sound. Sound-absorbing banners were incorporated into the design to provide acoustic variability to cater for amplified events and performances requiring a shorter reverberation time.

Implementation of the design had numerous challenges as the project was heavily politicized, and having two acousticians on the design team with others in the wings created some tensions. Also the architect, Jean Nouvel, when accused of cost overruns and delayed completion, took legal action against the Philharmonie, claiming that the finished concert hall was non-compliant with his original design – he refused to attend the opening concert in 2015.

Despite these difficulties, Harold Marshall's bicameral concept was successfully implemented, albeit with some modifications, and the acoustics were highly acclaimed by eminent conductors such as Sir Simon Rattle, who enthused about 'playing one of the very early concerts in the Philharmonie de Paris and realizing this is one of the world's greatest acoustics'. A view of the completed hall is shown in Fig. 3.40.

Fig. 3.40 The Paris Philharmonie. (Courtesy Marshall Day Acoustics)

In terms of the Philharmonie de Paris meeting the acoustic brief, it has certainly introduced a new typology, the bicameral hall, and the key subjective attributes such as clarity, reverberance and loudness all seem to have been achieved. Its possible shortcoming, perhaps a predictable one, is that the seats behind the orchestra are less favoured in terms of sound quality, which is a common problem with surround halls.

Elbphilharmonie, Hamburg

The Elbphilharmonie is a 2,100-seat concert hall in Hamburg, Germany, which opened in 2017. It was built at the top of a twenty-six-storey warehouse, and is surrounded on three sides by the River Elbe. The main hall, the Grosser Saal, was designed as a concert hall for classical music; a smaller venue, the Kleiner Saal, was designed as a multipurpose hall. The resident orchestra in the Grosser Saal is the NDR Elbphilharmonie Orchestra. The architects were the Swiss firm, Herzog & de Meuron, and the acoustic consultant was Yasuhisa Toyota of Nagata Acoustics.

Toyota summarized the acoustical design in terms of two important issues: the room shape and the interior finish materials. The room shape includes the seating layout, the ceiling height, the room width, and details such as surface textures of the ceilings and walls. The key word of the design was considered to be 'intimacy', and to achieve this, the audience was to be as close as possible to the performers. Prior to the appointment of Nagata Acoustics, the decision had been taken that the hall should follow the 'vineyard' concept and not the 'shoebox', so the design was already set for a surround-type hall (Oguchi, Quiquerez and Toyota 2018).

To achieve acoustical intimacy it was necessary to provide effective early reflections, and these were created by forming walls around the audience seating, which was split up into groups. To provide reflections for the musicians so they were able to hear themselves and each other, a 15m (50ft) wide saucer-shaped canopy was suspended at a height

Fig. 3.41 The Elbphilharmonie, Hamburg.

Fig. 3.42 Surface diffusion on the walls and ceiling at the Elbphilharmonie.

of 15m (50ft) above the stage. The volume of the hall was set at 23,000m³ (30,000yd³) to ensure a sufficiently long reverberation time, which necessitated a particularly high ceiling, reaching 25m (82ft). The completed concert hall, shown in Fig. 3.41, was tested extensively by computer modelling and also in a 1:10 scale model.

A particularly notable feature of the design is the irregular surface texture over the complete walls and ceiling (Fig. 3.42). This has a seashell motif and provides high-frequency diffusion and the suppression of possible disturbing echoes. The depth of the surfaces ranges from 10 to 30mm (0.4 to 1.2in) in some areas, and 50 to 90mm (2 to 3.5in) in others. When completed, acoustical measurements were carried out in the hall, which showed an ample reverberation time of 2.3 seconds when unoccupied. This was predicted to reduce to a respectable 2.1 seconds when occupied.

Following the inaugural concert, the hall proved very popular with audiences, who were attracted not only by the music but by the architectural splendour of the building, whose viewing plaza provides spectacular vistas of the River Elbe and the city of Hamburg. However, some disquiet about the acoustics began to emerge, which was voiced by the conductors. Peter Ruzicka was quoted as saying 'The side

blocks suffer from a strongly shifted acoustic balance', whilst Marek Janowski said, 'I think I can say in all modesty that the Elbphilharmonie does not belong to the best concert halls in the world.' The eminent recording engineer, Cord Garben, considered the 'white skin' of the hall to be a 'sound killer'.

The criticisms came to a head when the renowned tenor Jonas Kaufman was heckled by audience members who shouted that they could not hear him, and some walked out. In response he vowed that he might not sing in the hall again (Kesting, V. *Frankfurter Allgemeine*, 08.02.2019).

It is likely that the most vociferous audience members who could not hear at Kaufman's concert were sitting behind the singer; this is yet another example of the shortcoming of surround halls that have a significant proportion of seats behind the stage. But there are also other acoustic features of the hall that require investigating, one of them being the so-called 'white skin', which may well be absorbing excessive amounts of high frequency sound.

In summary, the Elbphilharmonie has not met expectations acoustically, and has thrown some doubt on the acoustic potential of surround-type halls, in particular the sound in the seats behind the stage.

Chapter Four

The Acoustics of Theatres

THE FUNDAMENTAL AIM OF THEATRES IN acoustical terms is to ensure good intelligibility of speech in all the seats. Acoustical design is therefore less demanding than in the design of auditoria for music. In the simplest terms it is necessary for words, and in particular syllables, to be heard clearly and distinctly. The conditions for good speech intelligibility can be readily achieved outdoors in quiet conditions, but only up to a limited distance, as the sound level decreases fairly rapidly with increasing distance owing to spherical spreading.

To determine what this distance is in very quiet conditions, an experiment was carried out in the Mohave desert in 1932 by the distinguished acoustician Vern Knudsen (Knudsen 1932). His results are shown in the plot in Fig. 4.1, from which it can be seen that speech is intelligible up to 42m (138ft) in front of the speaker, 30m (98ft) to the side and 17m (56ft) behind.

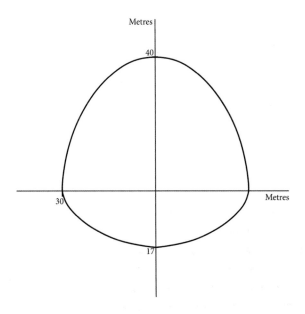

Fig. 4.1 Plot of the directionality of the human voice (after Knudsen).

The plot gives a good indication of the directionality of the human voice, and emphasizes the large decrease in intelligibility when the listener is behind the speaker. This is a particularly important point to bear in mind in the design of theatres, particularly those with an open-type stage (*see* later), where an actor will sometimes have his back towards part of the audience. Another aspect of this experiment is that when the background noise increased – even the noise produced by insects – the distances for intelligible speech decreased. This indicates the detrimental effect of background noise on speech intelligibility, another key design consideration.

It is worthwhile returning to our discussion on Greek theatre, as it involves speech in the open air.

Greek Theatre

Knudsen's experiment showed that speech can be intelligible in the open air up to 42m (138ft), so how was it possible in the Greek theatre at Epidaurus for members of the audience in the rearmost seats at 70m (230ft) to hear intelligible speech?

We have already shown that the direct sound between speaker and listener at Epidaurus is quickly followed by a strong reflection from the circular stage, or *orchestra*. This early reflection almost doubles the energy of the direct sound (an increase of 3dB), which compensates to some extent for the decrease in sound energy by spherical spreading. By assuming ideal conditions, Barron has suggested that this 3dB increase in early energy extends the distance where speech remains intelligible by a factor of 1.4 (Barron 2010). On this basis, listeners at Epidaurus as far distant as 60m (197ft) should receive intelligible speech. This was probably extended to 70m (230ft) by the actors wearing face masks, which amplified their speech to some extent.

The other factor, of course, was the low background noise level at this site. However, because of the directionality of the human voice, it is unlikely that the audience at the sides would be able to hear clearly at such far distances. As already mentioned, these seats were generally reserved for latecomers, foreigners and pregnant women.

The Acoustics of the Enclosed Theatre

When a space is enclosed there is a multitude of additional reflections compared with the outdoor situation. Some of these reflections will be early reflections arriving at the listener within 50ms of the direct sound. These early reflections will increase the clarity and intelligibility of speech, just as in the Greek theatre. However, the later reflections and the reverberant tail will act as noise, and will reduce intelligibility. The actual effect of the reverberation is to mask syllables that follow the initial syllable.

One might therefore surmise that no late reflections or reverberation are required. However, such a condition is not easily realized in an enclosed space, and even if it was, it would make the speech sound rather stark. Therefore, a controlled amount of reverberation is desirable, and generally it is recommended that the reverberation time in theatres is limited to 1 second.

Although this criterion is a useful guide for theatre design, it does not take account of the balance between the useful early reflections and the detrimental late reflections and reverberation. The criterion that does this is the 'early energy fraction', which has already been described in Chapter 1. This criterion expresses the proportion of the total energy arriving at the listener that is useful in increasing intelligibility. In general, it is considered that half of the total energy should be useful, so the fraction should be at least 0.5.

The challenge in designing a theatre is that the geometric design produces enough early reflections to achieve an early energy fraction of at least 0.5.

This is not a great challenge in small theatres, where the audience is close to the performers and therefore receiving a high level of direct sound. It is more of a challenge in large theatres seating 1,000 or more, where audience members are distant from the performers. Another major challenge is a result of the directionality of the human voice. In a theatre design where the actor is often facing away from sections of the audience, as in open stage theatres, the distance to the furthest seats has to be limited.

The first step in the acoustical design of a theatre is to set the reverberation time in the range 0.8 to 1 second, and to aim for a flat frequency response without a rise in the bass. The volume of the auditorium can then be determined by using the rule of thumb that recommends $4m^3$ ($5yd^3$) per seat. Larger volumes are possible but these would require the addition of acoustic absorption to reduce the reverberation time into the range 0.8 to 1 second. Although this is not inappropriate, absorption tends to reduce sound levels and may obscure useful early reflections.

In order to ensure that there are sufficient early reflections arriving in the audience area, surfaces need to be provided in front of the actor and orientated to direct reflections to the audience. In the proscenium type of theatre, such reflecting surfaces are readily provided at either side of the proscenium, and above and in front of the proscenium. The situation is difficult where the stage is more open, and reflecting surfaces can only be provided from above, either by suspended panels or the ceiling itself. Even then, the intelligibility of an actor will be reduced when the actor faces away.

Because the intelligibility of speech in a theatre tends to decrease with distance, it is important in designing theatres to limit the distance to the furthest seat. This distance limit will depend on the number of early reflections: the more such reflections, the greater the permissible distance. Also, it will depend on the form of the theatre: a proscenium theatre where most of the speech is delivered frontally can have a greater distance limit than a thrust stage theatre, where the actor often faces away from parts of the audience.

Bringing large audiences close to the stage involves the introduction of balconies. Although this means that some of the audience will be under balcony overhangs, the intelligibility of speech will be little affected, as the early sound will remain the same and the late sound will decrease. Thus deep balcony overhangs are acceptable in theatres, so long as sightlines are preserved. A typical nineteenth-century design using this principle will be discussed in the section on the Hackney Empire Theatre.

Barron has suggested some approximate limiting distances based on providing sufficient early energy and sufficient sound level arriving at the listener. For a proscenium theatre, the provision of two strong early reflections gives a distance limit of around 20m (65ft), taking account of the fact that the actor will sometimes be at 90 degrees to the audience. This distance aligns with visual requirements where there is a need to see the actor's expression. For theatre in the round, the distance limit reduces to 15m (50ft) to maintain the same level of intelligibility (Barron 2010).

The Early Proscenium Theatre

Teatro Olimpico, Vicenza

We have already mentioned the Teatro Olimpico in Vicenza, the oldest surviving Renaissance theatre, which was designed by Palladio and completed in 1585. The design has its roots in classical Greek theatre, but incorporates the contemporary artistic development of linear perspective. The audience area follows the classical curved plan and faces a large proscenium, behind which is a set forming the façade of a building with openings that give perspective views along streets, giving an illusion of depth (Fig. 4.2). The actors performed in front of the frontal façade, as otherwise they would look out of scale in the reduced dimensions further back. This, of course, kept them close to the audience, which was good for maintaining speech intelligibility.

This style of theatre, where the actors are on a type of forestage with separate scenery on a stage behind them, is a form that developed in the seventeenth century, and which is epitomized in the development of the English theatre in the Restoration and Georgian periods.

(a)

Fig. 4.2 Teatro Olimpico in Vicenza:
(a) auditorium,
(b) stage.

Fig. 4.2 *Continued.*

The Globe Theatre, London

Prior to the developments in theatre design in the seventeenth and eighteenth centuries, the Elizabethan theatre emerged in England, the most famous example being the Globe Theatre in London, built in 1599. Many of William Shakespeare's plays were written for this theatre, and subsequently performed in it. The Globe is considered of enormous importance in the development of English theatre, and this led to the recreation of the theatre in the twentieth century. It was constructed as authentically as possible, based on strong historical evidence and excavation of the original foundations; it was opened in 1996. A view of the rebuilt theatre is shown in Fig. 4.3.

The typical form of the Elizabethan theatre was approximately circular, with the large stagehouse on one side, and the stage projecting right up to the diameter of the circular plan. Two or three balconies were located around the perimeter, and joined on

Fig. 4.3 The reconstructed Globe Theatre. (Photo: Alamy)

to the stagehouse. The audience would either stand on the ground on the three open sides of the stage, or the more affluent members would sit in the balconies. This arrangement of the audience meant that it was virtually surrounding the stage and was therefore intimately involved with the action. This relationship was later diluted with the advent of proscenium theatres, but has been resurrected in the twentieth century with thrust stage designs (*see* later).

In acoustical terms, the Elizabethan theatre worked reasonably well, as most of the audience was close to the actors so that the direct sound was strong; the furthest seats would have been less than 25m (82ft) away. However, when an actor was facing away from parts of the audience, speech intelligibility was bound to drop in those parts. The absence of a roof meant that reverberation was almost non-existent, so there would be no degradation of speech intelligibility due to reverberance – but on the other hand, there would be little support from early reflections.

Theatre Royal, Drury Lane, London

Following on from the Elizabethan theatre and the hiatus in theatre performances during the interregnum between Charles I and Charles II, the development of theatre buildings in England in the seventeenth and eighteenth centuries was heavily influenced by the form of the Theatre Royal, Drury Lane, which was completed in 1663 but burned down in 1672. It was rebuilt and reopened in 1674 to a design carried out by the architect Sir Christopher Wren. Also influential was the theatre at Covent Garden, which was built not long afterwards in 1732. These two theatres, called 'patent' theatres, were the only ones in London permitted by law at that time to present plays.

The design of the Drury Lane theatre can be visualized from the reconstructed model by E. Langhans, shown in Fig. 4.4. This theatre design was seminal in the design of the majority of English theatres in the eighteenth century. The distribution of audience in these theatres consisted of a stalls area, called the pit, which was shaped like an elongated U, or a horseshoe or a fan, and was raked so that the rear seats of the pit were about level with the stage. Surrounding the pit was a row of boxes, and above these boxes there was a gallery in the centre. Above this gallery was an upper gallery, which extended along the sidewalls forming open balconies called 'slips'.

What is particularly interesting is that the stage extended right into the auditorium – in fact the stage comprised two parts: the forward part inside

Fig. 4.4 Model reconstruction of a playhouse, probably Drury Lane, by E. Langhans, after Nicoll. (Courtesy of Theatre Notebook, xviii, 3, 1963/4)

the auditorium where the acting took place, which was called the 'platform'; and the rear part where the scenery was placed, which was called the 'scene'. Therefore the theatre consisted of three parts: the 'house', the 'scene' and the 'platform'; this form is sometimes referred to as 'tripartite'. Actors on the platform were effectively in the same space as the audience – in fact some of the side boxes were actually within the platform area, so the audience here were extremely close. Actors and audience sharing the same space produced an intimate theatrical experience, where speech intelligibility was likely to be good because of the short distances involved.

A fine example of such a theatre form is the Theatre Royal at Bury St Edmunds, which was refurbished in 2007 and remains a fully active theatre.

Theatre Royal, Bury St Edmunds

The Theatre Royal in Bury St Edmunds was built rather late in the period, namely 1819, but it is a good example of Georgian theatre in terms of its form (*see* Fig. 4.5).

Although operating as a fully functioning theatre today, it was not always so, and for part of the twentieth century it was used as a barrel store by the brewers Greene King. Following a fund-raising exercise by the local community, the theatre was re-opened in 1965 and later leased to the National Trust, which carried out a major refurbishment between 2005 and 2007. The work involved restoring the building as closely as possible to its original design, with such changes as restoring the audience boxes, which had previously been removed.

The seating plan in the stalls follows the typical elongated 'U'-shape, which is surrounded by boxes. The seating capacity was originally 780, although this was reduced to 350 in the refurbishment owing to modern seating standards. The stage is extended to some extent in front of the proscenium following the 'tripartite' design.

In terms of acoustics, the reverberation time in the current theatre is close to 1 second, which is, as already stated, a good value for the spoken word. Also, the distances between stage and audience are not greater than 15m (50ft), which ensures that the direct sound remains strong. The only potential problem

Fig. 4.5 The Theatre Royal, Bury St Edmunds. (Courtesy Levitt Bernstein, architects for the refurbishment. Photo: Peter Cook)

involves the circular geometry, which is liable to cause focusing. This was dealt with in the refurbishment by treating sections of the curved walls with acoustically absorbent material.

Wilton's Music Hall, London

As we move from the Georgian to the Victorian era, another type of auditorium appeared: the music hall. These venues developed around 1850, and provided a different form of entertainment from drama. Performances involved popular songs, comedy, speciality acts and variety entertainment. The genre originated during the 1830s in public houses, and as their popularity increased some of these public houses were demolished and music hall theatres built in their place. The difference between music halls and theatres was that in the music hall the audience was seated at tables and allowed to drink and smoke.

A wonderful surviving example is Wilton's Music Hall in London, which underwent a major refurbishment between 2012 and 2014 (*see* Fig. 4.6). The hall has a relatively narrow rectangular plan with a barrel-vaulted ceiling, and currently seats 400, although it would have accommodated many more in its early days. There is a proscenium arch with a small stage area behind it, but typically a large forestage is arranged in front of the proscenium where action takes place. There is also a balcony that runs along three sides of the auditorium.

The hall had developed a reputation for good acoustics, which is not surprising because its narrow 'shoebox' shape provides strong early reflections that assist clarity, together with an ample volume to provide a degree of reverberance. The refurbishment brief was to preserve the acoustic quality and to reduce the ingress of external noise, which was dominated by the nearby railway. The external envelope was therefore upgraded, including a new roof and glazing. On completion, the mid-frequency reverberation time in the empty hall was measured as 2.3 seconds, an increase of only 0.1 seconds over its previous value. This value reduces to a little over 1 second with a full audience, which provides good acoustic conditions for the spoken word, singing and small music ensembles.

Fig. 4.6 Wilton's Music Hall. (Courtesy Tim Ronalds Architects. Photo: Helene Binet)

The Ascendancy of the Proscenium Theatre

Theatre design in the twentieth century was very much orientated towards the proscenium arch, with the audience on one side and the actors and scenery on the other. This style of creating a picture frame was partly influenced by the growth of cinema and the development of electric stage lighting. An early example is the Hackney Empire Theatre, which is described below. Later theatres in the modernist era adhered to the proscenium arch but omitted much of the lavish decoration.

Hackney Empire Theatre, London

The Hackney Empire Theatre, shown in Fig. 4.7, was designed by the pre-eminent and prolific Victorian theatre architect, Frank Matcham. It is considered one of his finest projects, and is described by Historic England as being 'one of the most exuberant Matcham interiors in Britain'. The theatre was completed in 1901 with the intention of providing a variety of acts for a wider audience than the earlier music halls. The auditorium seats 1,400, and the audience is brought close to the stage by the inclusion of three balconies. Matcham utilized the new technology of cantilevering balconies to avoid columns in the seating area, which would have obstructed views.

Matcham seems to have had an intuitive feel for acoustics, providing the right amount of reverberation in the auditorium by balancing the volume of the space with the number of people in the audience – the latter, of course, providing most of the acoustic absorption. The extensive and intricate decoration he introduced is useful for scattering incident sound, thereby creating a

Fig. 4.7 Hackney Empire Theatre. (Courtesy Tim Ronalds Architects. Photo: Martin Charles)

desirable diffuse sound field; the decoration also breaks up any strong late reflections that could be perceived as echoes.

The theatre was refurbished in modern times by Tim Ronalds Architects, and reopened in 2004. One of the key acoustical aims of the project was to preserve the natural acoustic. The reverberation time was measured during this period at around 1.5 seconds in the unoccupied condition; this would reduce to around 1.25 seconds when fully occupied. This is an ideal value for the performance of opera, and would have suited the Victorian variety performances, many of which involved singing and music. One of the features of the refurbishment was to create an orchestra pit capable of accommodating up to sixty musicians.

The refurbished Empire with its new pit has proved popular with opera companies such as English Touring Opera, as well as presenting a wide variety of performances ranging from comedy to music.

Olivier Theatre, Royal National Theatre

The proposal to build a national theatre was originally mooted in the nineteenth century, but it was not until 1948 that the London County Council proposed a suitable site on the South Bank near the Royal Festival Hall; this was followed by a 'National Theatre Act' passed by parliament in 1949 providing financial support. There was still considerable delay until the architect Denys Lasdun was appointed; the building was eventually opened in 1976.

The Olivier Theatre is the largest of the three main theatres in the building: it seats 1,160. It was modelled to some extent on the Greek theatre at Epidaurus, with a circular open stage, although the arc of the audience is limited to 90 degrees; this was considered by Sir Laurence Oliver himself to be a suitable geometry for providing an area of command for the actor – *see* plan and section in Fig. 4.8.

A view of the auditorium is shown in Fig. 4.9.

Although one might think that the adoption of the Greek theatre model with a limited fan angle might be a good acoustical approach, the design does not follow the fundamental principles of theatre design, and this has led to problems with speech intelligibility. Some of these problems have been mitigated over time, but others remain challenging. The first issue is the large volume of 13,500m³ (17,660yd³), or 11.6m³ (15yd³) per person, which is more than double the required volume of 4m³ (5yd³) per person. This excessive volume potentially leads to a long reverberation time, which is clearly detrimental to good speech intelligibility.

(a)

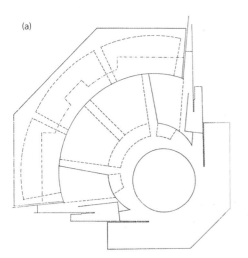

(b)

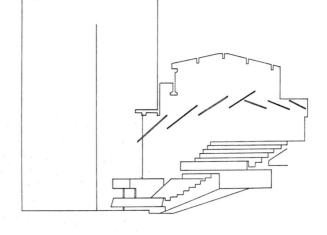

Fig. 4.8 Olivier Theatre: (a) plan and (b) section.

Fig. 4.9 Olivier Theatre auditorium, Royal National Theatre.

Secondly the distance from the stage front to the furthest seats is 25m (82ft); this would normally be 20m (66ft) for a proscenium theatre, but down to 15m (50ft) for an open stage configuration. These recommended distances assume at least one or two early reflections. Such early reflections could have been provided by the solid panels which the design incorporated into the ceiling, but both the forward panels above the stalls and the rear panels above the balcony were orientated at the wrong angle for this purpose.

A further complication was that the balcony front is a very pronounced arc of concrete, which focuses sound from the stage up to an overhead panel and then back to the stage, causing a disturbing echo. Other disturbing echoes occur in various locations from particular wall surfaces.

These shortcomings in the acoustical design were soon picked up by early audiences complaining of poor speech intelligibility, and led to prompt remedial measures. The worst case was when an actor faced away from part of the audience, leaving that section of the audience with poor intelligibility. Early reflections are very important in such situations and few were available.

Fortunately, an eighth-scale acoustic model of the theatre, which was being used for auditorium

research, was available in a laboratory at Cambridge University. The model was put to use to analyse the reported intelligibility problems and to recommend solutions. The disturbing echo on stage caused by the curved balcony front and an overhead panel was identified in the model, and eliminated by making the overhead panel acoustically absorbent; this treatment was then implemented in the theatre. At a later date this solution was switched to the balcony, which was in turn made acoustically absorbent.

Certain wall surfaces such as those to either side of the stage were also causing late echoes, and these too were made absorbent. A few of the echoes were identified as coming from unexpected surfaces, such as a corner between two walls, and placing a small amount of absorbent in such locations proved very effective.

The remedial measures developed using the scale model eliminated some of the immediate problems, predominantly echo problems, but the more fundamental problems were approached over several years and a number of them were gradually solved. For example, sound-absorbing material was introduced in the space above the ceiling panels, which helped to reduce the reverberation time; it is now around 1 second, which is an acceptable value. Some challenges still remain owing to the fundamental divergence of the acoustic design from fundamental principles.

The design of the Olivier Theatre was a move away from the traditional proscenium theatre, and was influenced by Sir Lawrence Olivier himself, who had been artistic director at the Chichester Festival Theatre, a venue with a thrust stage where the audience forms a 120-degree arc around the stage. The acoustics of the Chichester Festival Theatre have limitations because of the thrust-stage arrangement (Barron 2010), and show how important it is to provide plentiful early reflections in open-stage and thrust-stage designs.

Milton Keynes Theatre

Milton Keynes Theatre was designed and built at the end of the twentieth century and is a fine example of a civic theatre that has developed a strong reputation; a view of the auditorium is shown in Fig. 4.10. The architects were Blonski and Heard, who had previously designed the Theatre Royal Plymouth, amongst other auditorium projects. The brief for the theatre was to provide not only facilities for both intimate

Fig. 4.10 Milton Keynes Theatre. (Courtesy Blonski Heard Architects)

and large-scale drama, but also to cater for musicals, opera, ballet and orchestral concerts.

Each of these performance genres requires different acoustic conditions. Drama demands particularly high sound clarity for the spoken word. In opera this clarity needs to be balanced by a degree of reverberance to give fullness of tone to the singing voice and the orchestra. For orchestral concerts, yet more reverberance is required to give ample resonance to orchestral music.

These diverse acoustic requirements need extensive acoustic variability. To provide this in a positive and effective way, the auditorium ceiling, weighing 30 tonnes, was designed so that it can be raised and lowered by up to 10m (33ft). This enables the acoustic volume and sound reflection sequence to be adjusted to change the critically important balance between clarity and reverberance.

There are three pre-determined settings for the ceiling height; these are illustrated in the section diagram in Fig. 4.11. The lowest gives the minimum acoustic volume, which is appropriate for intimate drama; it also cuts off the upper circle, reducing the seat numbers from 1,400 to 900. The intermediate height provides a lyric theatre suitable for large drama, musicals and opera.

Fig. 4.12 Orchestra shell at Milton Keynes Theatre. (Courtesy Blonski Heard Architects)

The maximum height gives a concert hall with sufficient reverberance for full orchestral sounds. In this mode the orchestra is enclosed from above and behind by a concert shell to prevent the orchestral sound from being dissipated in the flytower, and instead to project it into the auditorium, see Fig. 4.12. The shell also provides reflections to help musicians hear each other. It consists of twelve towers, movable on air castors, together with an overhead reflector; all the surfaces in the shell are curved and faceted to direct sound to the players and the audience.

The architectural form, shown in an architectural model in Fig. 4.13, provides a largely 'frontal' audience arranged as front stalls and three tiers (balcony, circle and upper circle), and this provides the best possible sightlines. This is a good form for theatre, but not ideal for music as the fan form of the front side walls does not direct early reflections and early lateral reflections to the central seating area. To compensate for this, the geometrical form of the ceiling was designed to provide these reflections; a 1:50-scale acoustic model was used to optimize the reflection sequence.

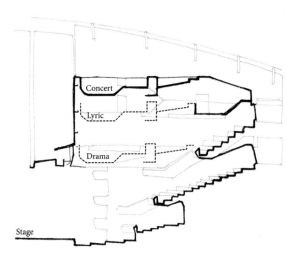

Fig. 4.11 Milton Keynes Theatre: section through the auditorium showing the three heights of the moving ceiling.

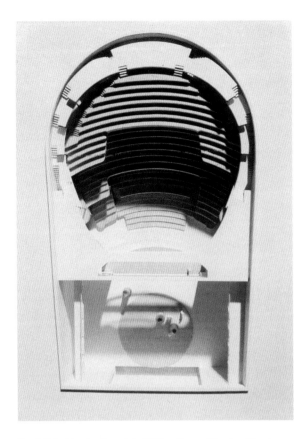

Fig. 4.13 Architectural model of Milton Keynes Theatre. (Courtesy Blonski Heard Architects)

Other surfaces in the auditorium were also specially shaped to reflect sound in useful directions. The balcony fronts were gently curved to avoid overly strong reflections, and the lower half was angled downwards to direct sound to the audience, *see* Fig. 4.14. Different angles were designed for balconies on different tiers, with angles getting steeper the higher up the auditorium.

The rear curved wall was fitted with convex panels to avoid focusing, *see* Fig. 4.15. Additional fine tuning of the acoustic is obtained by adjusting acoustic drapes on the side walls.

For opera performances, a suitable-sized pit can be formed by selecting an appropriate configuration of the three full-width stage lifts. The ceiling for opera performances is positioned at the middle setting, which gives a reverberation time of 1.25 seconds. This is similar to Glyndebourne Opera House and works very well for opera. The theatre has proved popular over the years with both Glyndebourne Touring Opera and Welsh National Opera.

The architects Blonski and Heard developed a bold design to meet the brief of a multipurpose civic theatre by employing a 30-tonne movable ceiling to cater

Fig. 4.14 Angled balcony fronts. (Courtesy Blonski Heard Architects)

Fig. 4.15 Convex diffusing panels on the rear curved wall. (Courtesy Blonski Heard Architects)

acoustically for the various functions. Their design decision has paid off, and audiences visiting Milton Keynes Theatre in the twenty-first century continue to enjoy a variety of top class performances with very good acoustics ranging from drama to opera.

The Contemporary Emergence of the Thrust Stage

The breakaway from the proscenium theatre was pioneered by Tyrone Guthrie, who first introduced a performance with a thrust stage at the Edinburgh festival in 1948 (Mackintosh 2011). His idea was to bring the action into the midst of the audience area and create an intimate relationship between the two. He went on to design a fully fledged thrust-stage theatre in Canada – namely, the Shakespeare Festival Theatre in Stratford, Ontario – and then a particularly successful version at Minneapolis. In England,

Guthrie's philosophy was adopted in the design of the Chichester Festival Theatre, although it was not an authentic thrust-stage arrangement. A more successful design was the Crucible Theatre in Sheffield, and also the Young Vic in London.

The trend in thrust-stage theatres gathered momentum with the restructuring of the Royal Shakespeare Theatre in Stratford-upon-Avon. Whilst in the original Stratford Theatre, which was a proscenium design of the modernist era, the distance from the stage to the rearmost seat was 30m (98ft), the distance in the new thrust-stage design is only 15m (49ft) for the same seat capacity. The volume of the auditorium was kept tight to control reverberation, and some of the wall panelling at ground level was tilted a few degrees to provide early reflections. The design has proved much more successful acoustically than its predecessor.

The most recent example of a thrust-stage theatre is the Bridge Theatre in London, which opened in 2017. It provides not only a thrust-stage design,

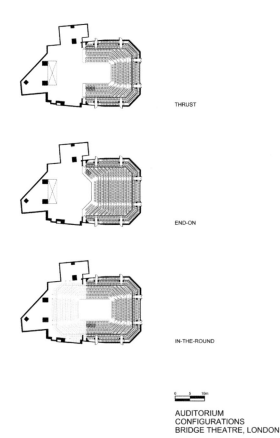

THRUST

END-ON

IN-THE-ROUND

0   5   10m

AUDITORIUM
CONFIGURATIONS
BRIDGE THEATRE, LONDON

Fig. 4.16 Configurations of the Bridge Theatre. (Courtesy Howarth Tompkins Architects. Photo: Philip Vile)

but can also be arranged in an end-on configuration and theatre-in-the-round, each arrangement seating around 900 audience. Fig. 4.16 shows the possible configurations.

In acoustic terms, both the thrust-stage arrangement and theatre-in–the-round need to provide an adequate number of early reflections to the audience, as the actors can face in any direction. This is challenging, as not many reflecting surfaces are available except for the ceiling. However, by keeping distances between actors and audience short, and controlling reverberation, good speech intelligibility is achieved.

The Bridge Theatre, pictured in Fig. 4.17, shows that it is possible within one space to cater for three main types of stage configuration: an end stage, a thrust stage and theatre-in-the-round. The latter two are more challenging acoustically than the former, but a carefully developed acoustic design can provide both good speech intelligibility and an intimate relationship between actor and audience.

Fig. 4.17 The Bridge Theatre, London. (Courtesy Howarth Tompkins Architects.

Chapter Five

The Acoustics of Schools

T HE HISTORY OF THE ARCHITECTURAL design of spaces for teaching probably goes back to Ancient Greek times, if not earlier. The acoustic design principles of the Greek theatre readily apply to contemporary teaching spaces – namely, a strong direct sound from speaker to listener, followed by short-delay early reflections. The Greek model persisted for many centuries, and, as has been seen in earlier chapters, when the seating area is covered over with a roof, many more reflections occur and the resulting reverberation time can become excessive.

In designing spaces for teaching, Sabine's theory, developed at the turn of the twentieth century, is essential for calculating reverberation time, although in the UK its uptake was slow. Practical applications of his theory to the acoustic design of rooms were described in a number of early twentieth-century textbooks, but references to the acoustic design of classrooms and school halls were rather limited. One of the better examples is the book by Bagnall and Wood entitled *Planning for Good Acoustics* published in 1931 – but even there the section on schools is limited to two pages (Bagnall and Wood 1931).

Developments in Acoustics in Schools in the Twentieth Century

Up to the 1920s there was virtually no consideration of acoustics in school buildings, where the Victorian plan still dominated; this plan was exemplified by a central assembly hall with classrooms grouped around it on all sides, the classroom doors opening directly off the hall (Fig. 5.1). A contemporary report about this type of layout commented that noise transmission between classrooms was intolerable at times (M.P.K. Keath 1983).

Matters improved in the 1930s, when a few pioneering designs – such as the design of Impington Village College by pioneering modernist architect Walter Gropius – took account of the environmental requirements of school buildings, including acoustics.

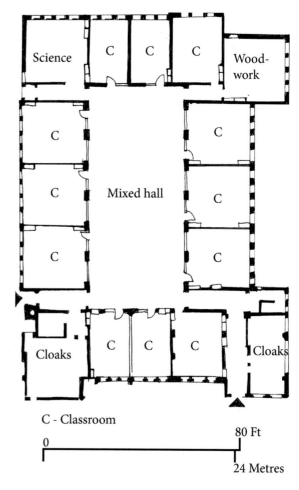

C - Classroom

0   80 Ft

24 Metres

Fig. 5.1 School layout based on the Victorian plan.

However, these developments were brought to a halt by the outbreak of World War ll.

After the war, the passing of the 1944 Education Act had a major influence on the design of school buildings. With this Act the Education Minister was required to prescribe by regulation the standards with which school premises should comply. Accordingly, in 1945 the Standards for School Premises Regulations 1945 came into formal operation. The standards were probably influenced by a report published by the Acoustics Committee of the Building Research Board of the Department of Scientific and Industrial Research (DSIR) entitled 'Sound Insulation and Acoustics' (HMSO 1944). This report covered school buildings and, interestingly, recommended that the sound reduction factor between classrooms should be '45db'. This is the very same standard as in the current regulations (*see* later), although the definition of the sound reduction factor is slightly different from the modern definition.

The overall aim of the Education Act was to prescribe minimum rather than maximum standards, with the intention of safeguarding rather than restricting design. A major intention of the Act was to enable the building of a large number of schools to cater for post-war needs in as economical a way as possible in the face of limited resources.

The building research branch of the DSIR – the Building Research Station, who contributed to the 1944 report – continued with the development of school design, and suggested a simple but very useful design aid for specifying the degree of sound insulation required between classrooms. Each classroom is classified by the amount of noise it makes, and its sensitivity to incoming noise (Parkin and Humphries 1963). This then leads to the formation of a nomogram, which indicates the desirable level of sound insulation. The nomogram is shown in Fig. 5.2.

For example, an ordinary classroom may be regarded as an average noise source with an average

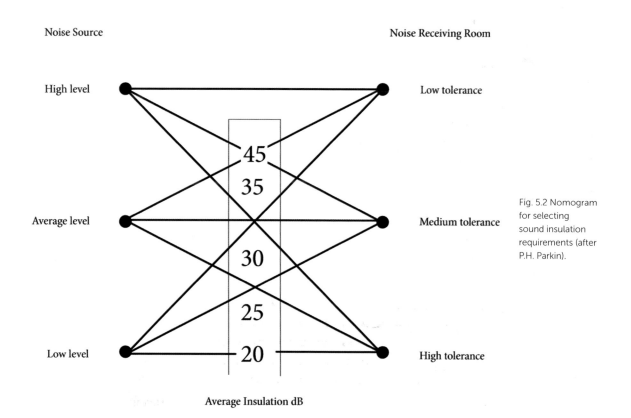

Fig. 5.2 Nomogram for selecting sound insulation requirements (after P.H. Parkin).

tolerance to incoming noise. By contrast, a music classroom is considered as a high-level source with low tolerance. This concept of categorizing classrooms was later used in the development of Building Bulletin 93: Acoustic Design of Schools, and is still a major feature in the current regulations (*see* later).

The Early Building Bulletins on Acoustics

The development of guidelines for acoustic design in schools was on a rather slow trajectory. For example, Building Bulletin 30, published by the Department of Education and Science in 1966, entitled 'Secondary School Design: Drama and Music', had a rather meagre section on acoustics, which showed that considerable confusion still existed. The following extract illustrates this:

> Many music teachers and other musicians feel strongly that the whole subject of acoustics in music rooms needs more careful study … At present there seems to be confusion even between the two very different functions of sound insulation and sound absorption.

There was some improvement in a subsequent publication in 1974 by the Department of Education and Science, which was entitled 'Guidelines on environmental design in educational buildings'. This document specified limits on background noise and also optimum reverberation times for different activities.

A significant step forwards came with the publication in 1975 of Building Bulletin 51 on the specific subject of 'Acoustics in Educational Buildings'. This was a detailed document describing the acoustic requirements of all types of teaching spaces in schools. It also contained detailed information about the sound absorption of various materials, and the sound insulation values of various types of construction. Although the design advice was not mandatory, the document set a benchmark for the acoustic design of schools and was the model for the later publication of Building Bulletin 93, which is now part of the Building Regulations and therefore mandatory.

With regard to educational facilities for those with hearing impairment, the British Journal of Audiology published a document in 1980 entitled 'Design of educational facilities for deaf children'. The recommendation in this document for a limit on noise from 'outside sources' was 35dBA, which compares reasonably well with the current standard of 30dBA (*see* later). The recommended limit for reverberation time was 0.5 seconds, which again compares favourably with the current limit of 0.4 seconds.

In 1981 a much shorter document was published by the Department for Education and Employment: it was called Design Note 17 with the title 'Guidelines for Environmental Design and Fuel Conservation in Educational Buildings'. This provided only the basic requirements in terms of acoustics, and was not a particularly favoured document, as some of the acoustic units were not standard ones.

This document was subsequently replaced in 1997 by an entirely revised version called Building Bulletin 87: Guidelines for Environmental Design in Schools (Revision of Design Note 17); the publisher was now called the Department for Education and Employment.

This document may be considered as the first to set out robust acoustic specifications for permissible background noise and minimum sound insulation between rooms. Values for reverberation times are also given. The readers are reminded that both existing and new schools are required by law to comply with the minimum standards prescribed in The Education (School Premises) Regulations 1996. These regulations state that each room or other space in a school building shall have the acoustic conditions and the insulation against disturbance by noise appropriate to its normal use. Thus, although it is not an absolute requirement to meet the acoustic standards in Building Bulletin 87, the guidance therein is showing signs of becoming mandatory.

Fig. 5.3 Chronological progression of Building Bulletins related to acoustics in schools.

Building Bulletin 87 was published together with a sister document Building Bulletin 86: Music Accommodation in Secondary Schools. This document will be discussed in the next chapter.

Although Building Bulletin 87 was considered by the Department of Education to be a valuable document, the department favoured a more comprehensive guidance document along the lines of the former Building Bulletin 51. Acoustic surveys of school buildings that were initiated for the update of Building Bulletin 87 were therefore extended to include detailed case studies. In parallel with these surveys, comprehensive guidelines were drafted on acoustic design, together with detailed examples on acoustic constructions and data on acoustic materials. These tasks, which included requirements for hearing-impaired pupils and those with special educational needs, involved wide-ranging expertise, and so a committee was formed that was chaired by an experienced acoustician in education, Professor Bridget Shield.

The completed document, Building Bulletin 93, was published by the Department of Education and Skills in 2003, and has created a seismic shift in the acoustic standards in all new schools and also in refurbished schools. The chronological progression of Building Bulletin publications is shown in Fig. 5.3.

The reason for this fundamental improvement is that Building Bulletin 93 is incorporated into the Building Regulations and is therefore mandatory. For a school to meet the Building Regulations, it must show compliance with Part E of Schedule 1 to the Building Regulations 2000 (as amended by SI 2002/2871) – in particular it must demonstrate that all performance standards given in Section 1.1 of the Building Bulletin have been met.

Building Bulletin 93 (BB93): Acoustic Design of Schools. A Design Guide

Setting the Standards

The aims of BB93 are clearly stated in the introduction, as follows:

- to provide a regulatory framework for the acoustic design of schools in support of the Building Regulations
- to give supporting advice and recommendations for the planning and design of schools

- to provide a comprehensive guide for architects, acousticians, building control officers, building services engineers, clients, and others involved in the design of new school buildings

Section 1 of BB93 sets out the acoustic standards that need to be achieved to meet the Building Regulations. These standards are quoted as being minimum standards, although it is clear that they are tighter than earlier ones and reflect the general recognition that teaching and learning are acoustically demanding activities.

The standards did not apply to alteration and refurbishment work in the first publication, although it was encouraged that such work should endeavour to meet them. Refurbishment work was later included in the revised version of BB93 published in 2015 (*see* later).

Sections 2 to 7 of the document are not part of the regulations, but give very detailed guidance on acoustic design aimed at meeting the standards in Section 1; in essence these sections are like a mini textbook on acoustic design of schools. The sections cover the following topics:

- Noise control
- Sound insulation
- Design of rooms for speech and music
- Design for pupils with special hearing requirements
- Case studies

Numerous appendices provide further valuable information, such as example calculations of sound insulation, reverberation time and absorption, together with example submissions to Building Control.

Section 1 starts by setting out the limits for the ambient noise levels in the various types of classroom; these are formally called the 'internal ambient noise levels' (IANL). Examples of limits for common types of teaching spaces are shown in Table 1. Note that each space is categorized by its tolerance to external noise, and how much noise it produces itself.

In addition to setting noise limits, Table 1, in conjunction with Table 2, can be readily used to evaluate the sound insulation required between teaching spaces, in a similar way to the nomogram proposed by Peter Parkin of the Building Research Establishment some years earlier. Table 2 is, in fact, an alternative way of presenting that nomogram in tabular form.

As an illustration, a classroom has low tolerance to noise and produces average activity noise; from Table 2, the value for the required sound insulation can be seen to be 45dB. By contrast, an assembly hall has low tolerance to noise and produces high activity noise. In this case the table gives a sound insulation value of 55dB. Note that the sound insulation is given as a level difference, D, which is measured on site; the subscript w indicates that the results in the individual octave bands are weighted to give a single number value; the result is also normalized to the maximum permissible reverberation time indicated by subscript $nT(T_{mf,max})$.

Table 1: IANL limits for common types of teaching space

Type of room	Activity noise (source room)	Noise tolerance (receiving room)	Upper limit for indoor ambient noise level $L_{Aeq,30mins}$ dB
Classroom	Average	Low	35
Science laboratory	Average	Medium	40
Music classroom	Very high	Low	35
Assembly hall	High	Low	35

Table 2: Standards for airborne sound insulation between spaces

Minimum $D_{nT(Tmf,max),w}$ (dB)		Activity noise in source room			
		Low	*Average*	*High*	*Very high*
Noise tolerance in receiving room	High	30	35	45	55
	Medium	35	40	50	55
	Low	40	45	55	55

In order to avoid the need for high sound-insulation values for the building envelope, and also to permit, where possible, natural ventilation, guidance is given in Section 2 on the selection of sites for schools in terms of acceptable external noise levels. Section 2 also gives advice on the internal planning of spaces to avoid the need for partitions with high sound insulation. For example, a buffer space such as a storeroom between a noise-producing space and a noise-sensitive space can avoid a high sound-insulating partition (*see* Fig. 5.4).

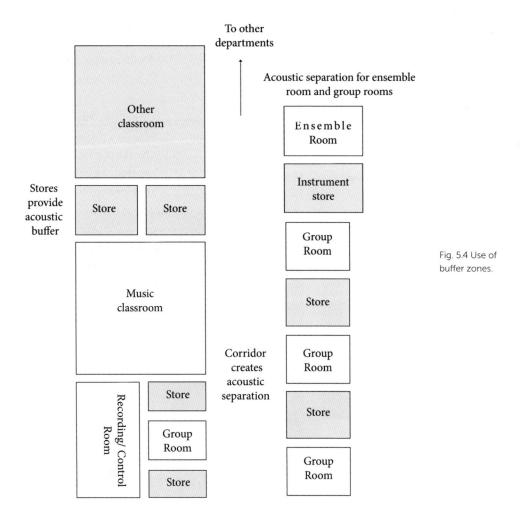

Fig. 5.4 Use of buffer zones.

Walls to Circulation Areas

Where a wall of a classroom is adjacent to a circulation area and contains a door, the sound insulation is specified in terms of laboratory values as it is difficult to measure accurately on site the sound insulation between rooms and corridors, or rooms and stairwells. For a standard classroom the sound insulation of the wall needs to be 40dB R_w and that of the door 30dB R_w. If the wall contains glazing and ventilators, then the composite sound insulation of the whole construction has to meet a specified standard.

A good example of such walls is shown below, where it has been possible to design the wall between classroom and circulation almost entirely of glazed panels (*see* Fig. 5.5a). This enables people moving about the circulation spaces to see the activities in the classrooms without causing any disturbance.

Similarly, passers-by are not disturbed by noise from the classrooms, and can converse or sit down and study without distraction (*see* Fig. 5.5b). Note that the circulation space or atrium has extensive sound absorption on the soffit to keep noise levels under control. The design of a fully glazed wall requires careful attention to detail in terms of the sound insulation of the glazing, the acoustic seals on doors, and the sound attenuation of the ventilators. These ventilators have special acoustic linings which reduce sound levels whilst enabling the passage of air.

Control of Impact Noise

The annoyance caused by footfall noise and furniture movement on upper floors is covered by specifying a maximum impact sound pressure level; this is the sound pressure level in a room where impact noise is being generated in the room above. Section 3 then gives advice about the type of floor constructions required to meet the specified limit. This may involve including a resilient layer in the floor build-up, such as in a floating floor construction (*see* Fig. 5.6) or adding a suspended ceiling.

Control of Reverberation

To ensure good speech intelligibility in teaching and study spaces, reverberation times are specified for a comprehensive range of rooms. A selection is given in Table 3.

Fig. 5.5 (a) Classrooms and laboratories are undisturbed by noise from a central atrium by sound-insulating glazed walls; and (b) circulation and study in the central atrium is not disturbed by noise egress from teaching spaces. (Architect: Tim Ronalds Architects. Photo: Helene Binet)

Floating floor using resilient pads or strips (such as 15mm tongue-and-groove floorboards on a 15mm plywood, chipboard or fibre-bond board on 50mm thick open-cell foam pads).

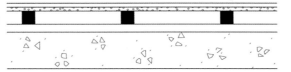

Fig. 5.6 Floating floor construction to control impact noise.

Table 3: Performance standards for reverberation in teaching and study spaces

Type of room	T_{mf} (seconds)
Nursery school quiet rooms	<0.6
Secondary school classrooms	<0.8
Open-plan teaching areas	<0.8
Music classroom	<1.0
Classrooms designed specifically for use by hearing-impaired students	<0.4
Assembly halls	0.8–1.2
Indoor sports halls	<1.5

To achieve these reverberation time values, a significant amount of sound absorptive material needs to be installed – typically an area equivalent to the floor area. This led to a number of different techniques for providing this absorption. One technique is to suspend absorbent panels or baffles from the ceiling, as shown in Fig. 5.7. These panels are a little more efficient at absorbing sound at high frequencies than fixing panels directly to the ceiling, as both sides of the panel are exposed to incident sound (*see* Fig. 5.7).

A variation of this arrangement is to suspend the panels as free-hanging rafts below the ceiling; these are illustrated in Fig. 5.8.

A further variation is to combine the rafts with light fittings, where the light element forms a central spine with wings either side that contain sound-absorbing material.

Another popular sound-absorbing treatment is to use hit-and-miss timber battens backed by a layer of mineral wool. The gaps between the battens should have an open area of at least 20 per cent of the total area to ensure a high level of sound absorption. A hall with this treatment can be seen at King's College School, Wimbledon (*see* Fig. 5.9).

Open-Plan Classrooms

The acoustic requirements for open-plan classrooms were known to be challenging, and the authors of BB93 were minded to discourage the use of such

Fig. 5.7 Suspended acoustic baffles to control reverberation in a classroom. (Architect: Allies and Morrison. Photo: Nick Guttridge)

Fig. 5.8 Suspended horizontal rafts to control reverberation in a communal area. (Architect: Tim Ronalds Architects. Photo: Helene Binet)

Fig. 5.9 Sound-absorbing treatment in a school hall. (Architects: Allies and Morrison. Photo: Nick Guttridge)

time that would help to provide a workable acoustic environment.

The criterion specified was a 'good' level of speech intelligibility for each teaching group, as expressed by the Speech Transmission Index, which was required to be greater than 0.6 (the index ranges from 0 to 1). From an acoustics point of view, an open-plan classroom with several different teaching activities occurring at the same time is likely to result in high noise levels and a distraction to study. One solution proposed in BB93 was to include operable walls within the open-plan area, so the overall space could be subdivided to provide more controlled acoustic conditions if the teaching required it. Although this was a possible solution to the open-plan issue, it was seldom adopted owing to the high cost.

It proved tricky to attempt to demonstrate that the criterion for speech intelligibility had been met using acoustic computer modelling, as advised by BB93, as the high noise levels assumed in an open-plan configuration often made it difficult to reach the required value of the Speech Transmission Index. It became clear in practice that the acoustic requirements of open-plan classrooms are complex, and that meeting the criteria of reverberation time and the Speech Transmission Index would not provide suitable acoustic conditions in all teaching arrangements.

spaces, although the educational trend was to promote them. Nevertheless, it was important to specify a parameter in addition to reverberation

Testing

To demonstrate to the Building Control Body that the acoustic design of a school was compliant with the building regulations, it was necessary to submit a set of plans, construction details, material specifications and calculations. When approved, along with other approvals, construction could proceed, although there was no guarantee that the acoustic performance would meet the design on completion. Therefore, BB93 recommended that the building contract should include a requirement to carry out acoustic testing to demonstrate compliance.

Revision of Building Bulletin 93

Updated Standards

Although BB93 led to a major improvement in acoustic conditions in new schools, a number of minor anomalies emerged as the document was put into practical use. The main problems identified were the difficulties in meeting the requirements in the following cases:

- Reverberation time in sports halls
- Criteria for open-plan teaching areas
- Sound insulation between classrooms with a personnel door in the separating wall (often required between laboratories)

- Sound insulation across operable walls (sliding folding partitions) between teaching spaces
- Sound insulation from kitchen to dining with a servery hatch in the separating wall

These anomalies were largely solved by the revision of BB93, which was published in 2015. The revised version is restricted to the mandatory performance standards (equivalent to Section 1 of the earlier document) and does not contain the guidance sections. These were produced as a separate document by a joint committee of the Institute of Acoustics and the Association of Noise Consultants under the title 'Acoustics of Schools: a design guide', published in November 2015.

An important addition to the revised BB93 document was a set of criteria for refurbishment work in schools. This closed a loophole in the earlier document, and although the standards for refurbishment are set slightly lower, it ensured that all building work in schools would meet a minimum standard.

Examples of the standards for both refurbishment and new build are shown in Table 4, which is the same as the earlier table but with the refurbishment standards added. Note that for refurbishment work, ambient noise levels that are 5dB higher are permitted.

As before, Table 4 can be used to specify the sound insulation required between teaching spaces; Table 5 shows the values for refurbishment. Note that sound insulation requirements for refurbishment have been reduced by between 5dB and 10dB.

Table 4: Levels of activity noise, noise tolerance and IANL limits

Type of room	Activity noise (source room)	Noise tolerance (receiving room)	Upper limit for indoor ambient noise level $L_{Aeq,30mins}$ dB	
			New build	Refurbishment
Classroom	Average	Medium	35	40
Science laboratory	Average	Medium	40	45
Primary music classroom	High	Medium	35	40
Assembly hall	High	Low	35	40

Table 5: Refurbishment performance standards for airborne sound insulation between spaces

Minimum $D_{nT,w}$ (dB)		Activity noise in source room			
		Low	Average	High	Very high
Noise tolerance in receiving room	High	Not applicable	30	35	45
	Medium	30	40	45	45
	Low	35	40	50	50

Sports Halls

It is interesting to consider one of the main anomalies in the original BB93 in relation to meeting reverberation time criteria in sports halls. A common design approach was to introduce the required amount of acoustic absorption on the ceiling; this amount having been calculated from Sabine's equation. This was an obvious location and left the walls free for sports activities and equipment. However, the measured reverberation time in such cases typically turned out longer than was predicted, and despite following the theory, the reverberation time criterion was not met.

The reason is that the tall hard walls of a sports hall provide plenty of opportunity for sound to reflect backwards and forwards horizontally thus increasing the reverberation time beyond the predicted value. To resolve this, it became clear that it is necessary to deploy part of the absorption on the walls and this guidance was provided in detail in *Acoustics of Schools: a design guide* (Institute of Acoustics and the Association of Noise Consultants; joint publication, 2015); a sketch showing this guidance is shown in Fig. 5.10.

In addition, the revision of BB93 linked the maximum reverberation time permissible to the size of the hall with larger halls (greater than 530m³ (693yd³) in floor area) permitted to go up to 2 seconds. A knock-on effect of this guidance was that acoustically absorbent materials were required that were impact resistant, and the manufacturers were prompt in developing such materials. These materials have the usual acoustically absorbent core of mineral wool but are faced with a robust perforated cover.

Halls with Shallow-Pitched Ceilings

A similar acoustic anomaly arises in halls with a shallow-pitched ceiling. This can be best illustrated

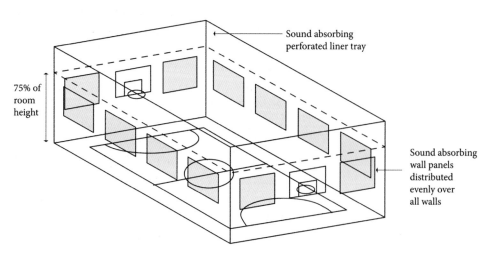

75% of room height

Sound absorbing perforated liner tray

Sound absorbing wall panels distributed evenly over all walls

Fig. 5.10 Recommended deployment of acoustic absorption in a sports hall.

by an example of a multi-purpose hall in a county primary school built in the early 1990s. Activities in the hall include assemblies, singing, concerts and physical education. Teachers reported acoustical problems soon after the hall opened. In particular they complained of poor speech intelligibility, which they could only marginally improve by speaking slowly. Interestingly, they found that addressing groups of pupils from a sidewall rather than near the centreline was better. Speech from the centreline of the hall appeared louder than normal, and sounded coloured or distorted. Furthermore, noise levels near the centreline appeared unusually high, for example the noise of children shuffling their feet.

The main cause of the problem was the shape of the ceiling, which has a shallow pitch of around 5 degrees with hipped ends, similar to a shallow vault. Both the ceiling and the floor below are hard timber surfaces and so highly reflective to sound. A section of the hall is shown in Fig. 5.11.

Sound generated in the hall, particularly near the centre line, was reflected by the shallow-pitched ceiling and then incident on the floor below. The floor would then reflect the sound back up to the ceiling, which would then focus it back to the source position, and the process would repeat itself. This backwards and forwards sequence of reflections prolonged the reverberation and increased sound levels.

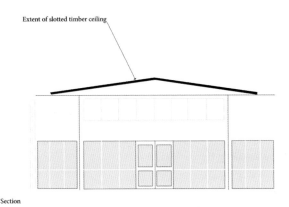

Fig. 5.11 Section of the school hall with shallow-pitched ceiling.

To rectify the fault, the ceiling was made acoustically absorbent. This reduced the reverberation time for primary school uses and reduced the focusing effect. Although it provided a solution in this case, it is not normally advisable for ceilings to be sound absorbent in rooms where good speech intelligibility is a requirement. If the size, shape and geometry of the space is right, the ceiling should be reflective to sound, at least in the central area. The reason for the success of the ceiling treatment in this case was the overriding need to make a substantial reduction in the reverberation time.

The school was particularly keen to retain the timber ceiling, and so the timber boards were perforated with slots, providing an open area of approximately 25 per cent: the pattern of the slots is illustrated in Fig. 5.12. A mineral-wool quilt 25mm thick was laid directly over the slots in the ceiling void, providing the acoustic absorption.

The acoustic treatment to the timber ceiling was considered to retain the aesthetic appearance of the hall, and the response of the teachers to the modified acoustics was very favourable; all reported a very noticeable improvement. The hall following acoustic treatment is shown in Fig. 5.13.

Speech intelligibility was found to be much improved when addressing both small and large groups of children, and the noise from physical activities and from children shuffling their feet during assembly was substantially reduced.

The reverberation time was measured before and after the remedial work, including source and receiver positions on the centreline and near a sidewall. The results are shown in the graph below (see Fig. 5.14), where it can be seen that the reverberation time before treatment reaches a very high peak of nearly 4 seconds on the centreline. By contrast, the peak reverberation time at the side is significantly lower, at 2.7 seconds. This confirms that the focusing effect causing multiple reflections occurs mainly around the centreline. Following treatment, the mid-frequency reverberation time falls to around 1 second, which meets the BB93 requirement.

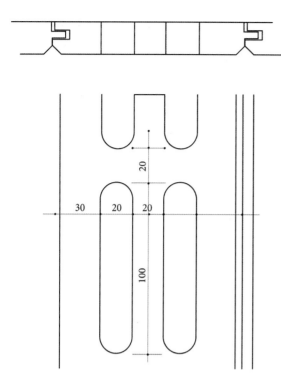

Fig. 5.13 The school hall following acoustic treatment to the ceiling.

Fig. 5.12 Detail showing perforations in the timber ceiling. Dimensions in mm.

Fig. 5.14 Measured reverberation times in the school hall before and after acoustic treatment.

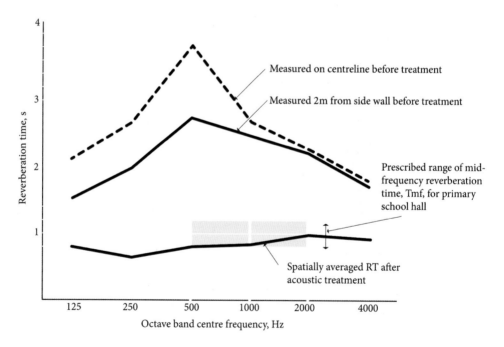

In general, acoustic treatment in school halls to control reverberation time should be evenly distributed on the walls and ceiling. However, in this special case of a shallow-pitched ceiling causing serious focusing, deployment of absorption on the ceiling was the right solution. A corollary is that shallow-pitched ceilings, vaults and domes should be avoided in the design of halls, as the resulting focusing effect can be difficult to deal with.

Open-Plan Classrooms

Another interesting and challenging anomaly, as discussed earlier, was meeting and measuring the criterion of the Speech Transmission Index for open-plan classrooms. The requirements for the Speech Transmission Index were expanded to include a suitably low value between different teaching groups, as well as a high value within the group itself. These values are shown in Table 6.

Table 6: STI performance standards for speech intelligibility and privacy in open-plan spaces

Condition	Speech Transmission Index (STI)
Instruction or critical listening activity – within group	≥0.6
Between groups (during critical listening activities)	≥0.3

However, these performance standards were excluded from the Building Regulations but were incorporated into the School Premises Regulations, so the computer modelling and related justifications still have to be carried out and submitted to Building Control.

THE IMPACT OF BB93 ON SCHOOL DESIGN

There is no doubt that BB93 has had a huge impact on the design of schools, and has effectively raised the acoustic conditions in all new schools and refurbished schools to a good standard. It has also changed the mind-sets of people throughout the building industry, many of whom previously considered acoustics as an expensive and often an optional add-on. Now, architects, engineers and contractors are all familiar with the requirements and are aware that they have to be met.

In visual terms, the most evident feature is the deployment of acoustic absorption, which has provided architects and designers with opportunities to introduce a new dimension into educational buildings, as shown in Fig. 5.15.

Fig. 5.15 Acoustically absorbent panels introducing a variety of form into a school environment. (Photo: Tom Jones)

Chapter Six

Music Schools and Recital Halls

IN THE PREVIOUS CHAPTER ON SCHOOLS, it was perhaps surprising to note that even as late as the 1960s, the understanding of the acoustical requirements for music schools was confused. This was exemplified by a comment in Building Bulletin 30 entitled 'Secondary School Design: Drama and Music' published in 1966 by the Department of Education and Science (*see* Ref). The comment is repeated here in full to illustrate how uninformed the approach could be to music school design:

> Many music teachers and other musicians feel strongly that the whole subject of acoustics in music rooms needs more careful study ... At present there seems to be confusion even between the two very different functions of sound insulation and sound absorption. Often, in an attempt to 'sound proof' a music room, all kinds of absorbent materials are applied to walls and or ceiling to deaden the sound at source. This is the last thing that singers or players want: they want to hear and appreciate the sounds they create, and for this the room must have resonance.

Some progress was made with the publication in 1975 of Building Bulletin 51 (*see* Ref) on the specific subject of Acoustics in Educational Buildings but the major step forward with regard to music accommodation came in the 1990s when the Department for Education and Employment commissioned a survey of music facilities in schools in England.

The survey led to the publication in 1997 of Building Bulletin 86 entitled 'Music accommodation in secondary schools: a design guide' (DfEE 1997).

This document had a detailed section on acoustics and provided guidance on the design of music classrooms, recital rooms, group rooms and recording facilities. It also included a number of exemplary case studies.

This document was considered a valuable addition to publications on the acoustic design of schools, and following a decade in use it was revised and expanded and reissued in 2010 under the guidance of the Department of Education under the same title. It is now cited in the revised version of Building Bulletin 93 (DfE 2015), which refers to it for additional guidance on acoustics in music accommodation.

Fundamental Acoustic Requirements for Music Accommodation

Music rooms must provide an acoustic environment that allows students to fully appreciate, without disturbance, the activities of playing, listening and composing. These activities take place in a range of spaces including music classrooms, practice rooms, ensemble rooms and recital halls. The three main aspects of a successful acoustic environment for a room where music is being played are:

- The control of ambient noise to a suitably low level
- The provision of adequate sound insulation from other sources of sound that could cause disturbance
- The provision of good acoustics within the space for singing and instrument playing

Control of Indoor Ambient Noise

The indoor ambient noise may be dominated either by external noise or by building services noise, or it may be a combination of the two. Specific limits are, of course, set out in Building Bulletin 93.

For spaces that are naturally ventilated, usually via open windows, external noise is likely to be dominant because of the large openings required. If the music department is in a quiet location, noise ingress through the natural ventilation openings is likely to be acceptable.

In noisier locations, where the external ambient level is above 50 dBA, natural ventilation openings will require acoustic attenuation to reduce noise ingress to prescribed levels. The attenuation can be provided by tortuous inlets and outlets that are lined with acoustically absorbent material. The type of attenuator will need to be matched to the amount of noise reduction required. The principle of an attenuator of this type is shown in Fig. 6.1.

If the external ambient levels are higher than 70dBA, then natural ventilation is not feasible and mechanical ventilation is necessary. To control noise from mechanical ventilation requires the selection of quiet fans that are connected to appropriately sized silencers.

Other building services can also cause disturbance, such as noise from hot water radiator systems. Care has to be taken to mount pumps on anti-vibration mounts and to select valves for quiet operation.

Sound Insulation

Sounds that may cause disturbance to a music room include:

- Music from adjacent rooms
- Movement of people in adjacent circulation areas
- External noise such as road traffic noise
- Plant noise

Standards for sound insulation between different types of music room are given in Building Bulletin 93. To avoid excessive transfer between music rooms, the Bulletin specifies a minimum sound level difference of 55dB between most music rooms. These are minimum requirements and will not always prevent interference between adjacent rooms. It is beneficial to increase this figure, say to 60dB, particularly when the indoor ambient level is significantly below the specified level in Building Bulletin 93 – that is, below 30dBA. This can occur in naturally ventilated rooms on quiet sites where the indoor ambient noise level is too low to provide useful masking of distracting noise from adjacent rooms.

To achieve a sound level difference of 55dB between adjacent music rooms it is necessary to introduce some isolation between them to reduce the transmission of sound. The simplest way of achieving this is to employ a box-in-box construction, where the inner box is structurally isolated from the main structure. Fig. 6.2 shows the principle of a box-in-box construction where a concrete

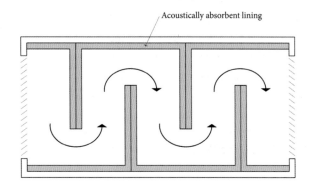

Fig. 6.1 A sound attenuator to control noise ingress.

Acoustically absorbent lining

Air vent outside

Air vent inside

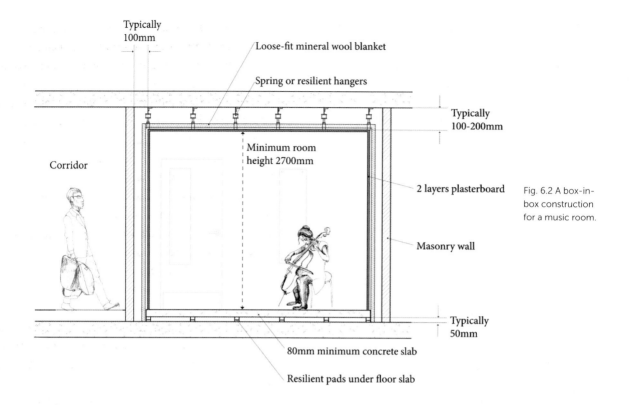

Typically 100mm

Loose-fit mineral wool blanket

Spring or resilient hangers

Corridor

Minimum room height 2700mm

Typically 100-200mm

2 layers plasterboard

Masonry wall

Fig. 6.2 A box-in-box construction for a music room.

Typically 50mm

80mm minimum concrete slab

Resilient pads under floor slab

or multi-boarded floor is supported on resilient mounts (this is called a floating floor) and a heavy plasterboard room is built off this floor; this inner room is completely isolated structurally from the main building structure.

It is particularly important to consider rooms for percussion and brass because they generate high noise levels and tend to cause the most disturbance in music schools. Care is therefore needed in choosing their location; percussion rooms, in particular, should be located at ground level to minimize the transmission of impact noise into the building structure, which can then radiate throughout the building. Box-in-box constructions should always be used for percussion rooms, especially drum rooms, and the level of sound insulation with adjacent rooms should be increased to 60dB. Also, doors into percussion rooms should be lobbied, as shown in Fig. 6.3.

The principles of good planning, where corridors and storage areas are used as buffer zones

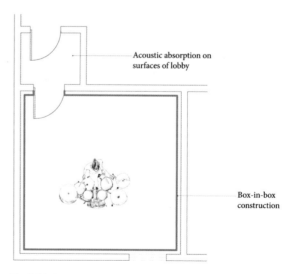

Acoustic absorption on surfaces of lobby

Box-in-box construction

Fig. 6.3 Lobbied doors to percussion rooms.

between music rooms, were described in the previous chapter. This allows the sound-insulation requirements to be met without resorting to high performance constructions.

Noise in circulation areas, such as animated talking and shouting, must be controlled to avoid disturbance. However, limited leakage of musical sounds into circulation routes is acceptable, since it allows teachers to monitor activities and is often desirable for attracting people to music.

Room Acoustics

Control of Reverberation Time

The quality of sound in a music room should be an appropriate balance between clarity and reverberance with a suitable level of loudness. The key factor in achieving this is the reverberation time. A long reverberation time promotes reverberance (and loudness) but at the expense of clarity (individual sounds start to overlap each other, reducing clarity). A short reverberation time tends to provide clarity but at the expense of reverberance: thus spaces with a very short reverberation time can have a 'dead' quality. For a typical music classroom the reverberation time should be a little less than one second.

As an example, in a typical practice room with a floor area of 8m² (9.6yd²) and a height of 2.7m (3yd), the resulting volume of 22m³ (29yd³) must be balanced by a total acoustic absorption of around 6m² (7m²) to achieve the prescribed reverberation time of 0.6 seconds for a practice room. The absorption can be provided by 4m² (4.8yd²) of acoustically absorbent panels distributed on the walls, together with a medium pile carpet (incidental absorption by furnishings and wall surfaces will add to the total required).

Room Geometry

In designing music rooms, it is important to consider both room shape and proportion. In large rooms, such as recital halls, the geometry and orientation of the room surfaces will determine the directions in which sound is reflected, and this, in turn, will determine the sequence of sound reflections arriving at the listener from a given sound source. Early reflections – that is, those arriving within approximately 1/10 second (80ms) of the direct sound – will be integrated by the listener's hearing system and will enhance the clarity of the original sound.

Prominent reflections with a longer delay (late reflections) may be perceived as echoes. This is often encountered where the rear wall in a hall has a large flat area of an acoustically reflective material such as plaster on masonry.

Strong individual reflections can also lead to 'image shifting', where early reflections can be so strong that the ear perceives the sound as coming from the reflecting surface rather than the sound source. This problem is exacerbated if late reflections are particularly strong. This can occur when sound is focused by large concave surfaces such as curved rear walls, barrel vaults and domes. Furthermore, focusing gives rise to an uneven distribution of sound throughout the room. Consequently, large concave surfaces are not generally recommended in music spaces.

In small rooms, such as music practice rooms, the geometry affects the distribution of standing waves or room modes, particularly at low frequencies. The occurrence of these modes was described in Chapter 1; they are caused when the distance between two parallel walls coincides with – or is a simple multiple of – a particular wavelength of sound.

The result is that certain notes will be amplified more than the rest, leading to an unbalanced tonal sound called 'coloration'. The effect is exaggerated if distances are the same in more than one dimension. Therefore rooms that are square, hexagonal or octagonal should be avoided. The same effect occurs if the room width is the same as the room height, or a simple multiple of it.

Ideally, the distribution and strength of room modes should be reasonably uniform throughout the sound spectrum. The best way to control the low frequency modes is to select room dimensions that are not simple ratios. It should not be possible to express any of the room dimensional ratios as whole numbers. For example, a proposed space 7m wide, 10.5m long and 3.5m high (2:3:1) would not be considered an advisable shape from an acoustic point of view. Mathematically, a good ratio is 1.25:1.6:1 (sometimes referred to as the 'golden ratio'), but many other ratios work equally well.

Room modes, and also flutter echoes, can be controlled to some extent by using non-parallel facing walls, but this is often impractical in terms of ease of construction. The use of angled panels, typically in zig-zag formation, fixed on the walls of parallel-sided rooms is an effective solution.

Diffusion of Sound

Diffusion is the process whereby sound energy is distributed around a room. A high degree of diffusion means that the sound is distributed evenly throughout the room, and this is generally desirable. A low degree of diffusion implies that the distribution is uneven, and there may be loud spots or quiet spots. This is generally undesirable: for example, concave walls can sometimes result in poor diffusion because of their focusing effect.

To promote good diffusion it is necessary to incorporate diffusing surfaces on the walls or ceiling of a room. Diffusing surfaces are simply irregularities or 'bumps' on a surface which scatter the incident sound in different directions. Diffusers may be curved convexly, angled or stepped. Fig. 6.4 shows the principles of diffusing surfaces.

The depth of the irregularities affects the wavelength of the sound scattered. A depth of 50mm affects only high frequencies, above approximately 2kHz, whereas a depth of 300mm affects bass frequencies around 300Hz. A patchwork of sound-absorbing panels can also provide diffusion because of special effects that occur at the edges around the perimeter of a panel (called diffraction), which tends to scatter sound.

The most important rooms where diffusion is required are practice rooms, where it is important to reduce the effects of standing waves and flutter echoes. These can cause an uneven acoustic quality and disturbing effects. To provide diffusion in practice rooms, it is recommended that one of the walls, usually the long wall, includes diffusing elements; these can be simply angled or curved panels of timber or plasterboard with a depth of typically 100mm. Greater depths up to 300mm are desirable, because they extend the diffusion to lower frequencies but they are not always practical in small rooms.

Diffusion on other walls in a practice room can be provided by shelving, furniture and other incidental objects. The photograph (Fig. 6.5) shows a typical practice room with timber diffusing panels. Angling one of the walls of a practice room by around 5 degrees may be of some use for promoting diffusion but a parallel sided room with diffusing wall elements can be equally effective.

Plane surface causes specular reflection

Simple angled panels - diffuse reflection

Curved panels - diffuse reflection

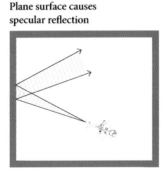

Fig. 6.4 Surfaces producing specular and diffuse reflections.

50–300mm (larger depth extends diffusion to lower frequencies)

50–300mm (larger depth extends diffusion to lower frequencies)

Fig. 6.5 Typical practice room with diffusing panels.

In larger practice rooms, music classrooms, recital rooms and halls, diffusing surfaces should be used on extensive plane surfaces such as large acoustically reflective walls, particularly rear walls, to diffuse incident sound that could otherwise cause a disturbing echo or reflection (Fig. 6.6).

Fig. 6.6 Recital room with diffusing panels.

Types of Music Space

Music Practice Rooms

Practice rooms for both individual practice and instrumental lessons need sufficient volume and should have a minimum plan area of 8m² (9.5yd²) and a minimum height of 2.7m (8.9ft).

The layout of a typical practice room is shown in the plan in Fig. 6.7. The angled panels or sound-absorbing panels are necessary to reduce the effect of standing waves and flutter echoes, as described above. An acoustic drape along one of the long walls can provide acoustic variability; when extended it will reduce the reverberance and loudness but enhance clarity. This may be desirable for certain types of loud instruments, brass for example, and it may also be useful for certain types of intense practice. Acoustic drapes do not use a specialized material and typically comprise two layers of heavy wool serge, each layer having a weight of 500g per square metre. The drapes are usually hung with at least 50 per cent gather, which means one-and-a-half widths of material.

In terms of surface finishes, carpet on the floor provides some useful sound absorption, whilst the other surfaces are hard and acoustically reflective to generate the required reverberation.

Percussion rooms and drum rooms, and also those for amplified music, can be very loud spaces and require extensive sound absorption to keep loudness levels under control. Therefore, these spaces should have sound-absorbing panels on all the walls and the ceiling, leaving only a small proportion of the room surfaces hard and acoustically reflective.

It is an advantage to keep the window of a practice room small to control the amount of external noise entering the space. Natural ventilation can be provided by opening this window when no noise disturbance is likely either by noise ingress or noise egress. However, when noise disturbance is a problem, the window can be closed and an alternative ventilation system used, for example by using acoustically attenuated inlet and outlet vents with fan assistance.

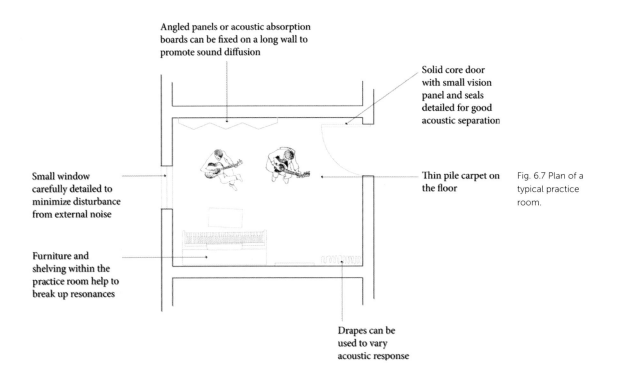

Angled panels or acoustic absorption boards can be fixed on a long wall to promote sound diffusion

Solid core door with small vision panel and seals detailed for good acoustic separation

Small window carefully detailed to minimize disturbance from external noise

Furniture and shelving within the practice room help to break up resonances

Thin pile carpet on the floor

Drapes can be used to vary acoustic response

Fig. 6.7 Plan of a typical practice room.

Large Music Practice Rooms

Large music practice rooms or ensemble rooms, with a floor area of 25m² (30yd²) upwards, will accommodate a dozen or so musicians. Such rooms should have a high ceiling of at least 3m (10ft), and should otherwise follow all the same acoustic design rules of smaller practice rooms in terms of sound absorption and diffusion.

Music Classrooms

The plan in Fig. 6.8 shows a typical music classroom with a floor area of 65m² (74yd²). It will accommodate a range of class-based activities including singing, composition, listening, music theory teaching, instrumental playing and keyboard use. The dimensions of the room should avoid multiples of each other, the worst of which would be a square. The height of the ceiling should be at least 3m (10ft), creating a reasonable volume for the various musical activities.

To minimize the possibility of flutter echoes between opposite parallel walls, surfaces are modelled to promote sound diffusion. This modelling can be provided automatically by fixed furniture such as shelving and desking, or, where this is not present, by diffusing or sound-absorbing panels. Standing waves will be less problematic in a larger room. Full-length acoustic drapes along one of the walls can provide acoustic variability, which can be used to suit the activity taking place.

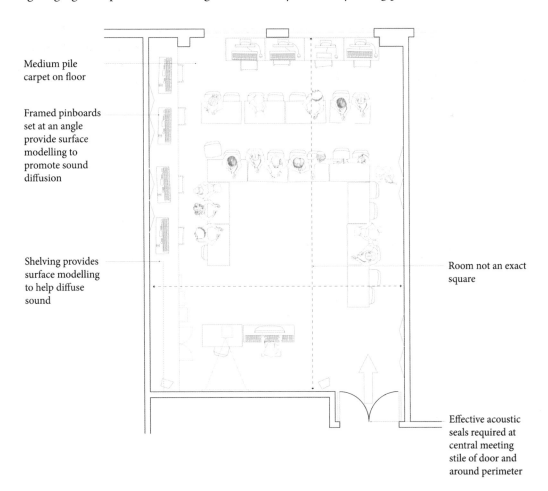

Medium pile carpet on floor

Framed pinboards set at an angle provide surface modelling to promote sound diffusion

Shelving provides surface modelling to help diffuse sound

Room not an exact square

Effective acoustic seals required at central meeting stile of door and around perimeter

Fig. 6.8 Plan of a typical music classroom.

Recording/Control Rooms

In a music school, a recording/control room will usually be used to record a music performance taking place in an adjacent studio or recital hall, after which the recording may be listened to on headphones or loudspeakers. The reverberation time needs to be short, less than 0.5 seconds, to ensure that the replay over loudspeakers is not distorted by the acoustics of the room. This is achieved by treating all available surfaces with sound-absorbing material; typically this will be 50mm-thick panels of fabric-faced mineral wool, together with carpet and acoustic ceiling tiles.

Observation windows between the control room and recording studio need to have high sound insulation, which requires double glazing with a large cavity between the panes. The two glass frames should be structurally separate, as illustrated in Fig. 6.9.

Recording Studios

The sizes of a recording studio will vary depending on the size of the musical ensemble being recorded. For a small studio in a music school, the size should be sufficient to at least accommodate a sextet with piano, or a rock band with full drum kit; dimensions of 5m by 4m (16 by 13ft) would be a minimum. The acoustic surface finishes in a studio are quite sophisticated as they need to provide a reverberation time with a flat frequency response across the whole sound spectrum; this requires a carefully designed mix of both porous absorbers and tuned panel absorbers; these devices can be up to 200mm (8in) thick.

There is also a need for sound diffusion to eliminate standing waves and strong reflections; sound diffusers will also have a similar depth. Therefore in the design, account must be taken of these deep surface finishes

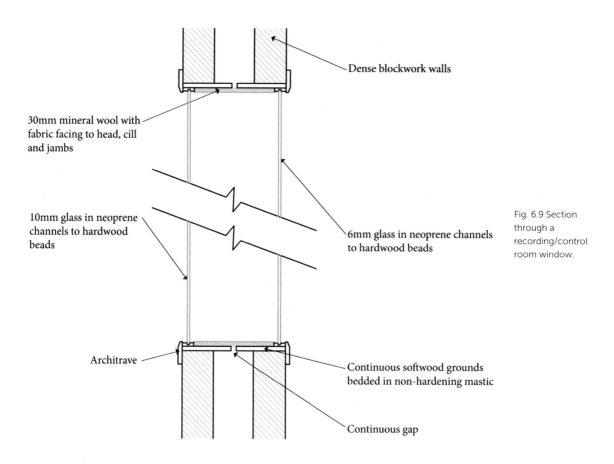

Dense blockwork walls

30mm mineral wool with fabric facing to head, cill and jambs

10mm glass in neoprene channels to hardwood beads

6mm glass in neoprene channels to hardwood beads

Fig. 6.9 Section through a recording/control room window.

Architrave

Continuous softwood grounds bedded in non-hardening mastic

Continuous gap

Fig. 6.10 A recording studio in a music school.

to ensure that sufficient studio space remains. Fig. 6.10 shows a recording studio with typically deep surface finishes. Very low ambient noise levels are, of course, required in a studio so that the envelope must have high sound insulation, often a box-in-box construction, and the ventilation noise must be highly silenced.

Recital Halls

Most music schools incorporate a recital hall where students can perform in front of an audience. The audience size of these recital halls can vary from around 100 to 500, depending on the requirements of the school. The general principles of the design of recital halls is set out below, followed by examples of different approaches to design.

General Design Principles of Recital Hall Design

The key acoustic requirements in recital hall design are sufficient volume to provide adequate reverberation, and a shape that will provide a uniform sound field.

A suitable volume for a recital hall is around 8 to $10m^3$ (9.5 to $12yd^3$) per audience member including musicians, which for a 350-seat hall would require a volume of around $3,000m^3$ ($3,590yd^3$). The target value for the reverberation time is around 1.5 seconds. The number of instrumentalists must also be considered, as sufficient volume is also required to achieve the appropriate balance between reverberance and loudness; $3,000m^3$ should accommodate an ensemble of up to thirty musicians.

In terms of shape, a rectangular plan is an excellent shape acoustically because the sequence of sound reflections from stage to listener is close to ideal, and because it is usually the least expensive to build and the most reliable in practice. Dimensions approximating to a double cube are good, giving rise to the traditional 'shoebox' shape.

A balcony helps to increase both visual and aural intimacy, and can also extend along the sidewalls. However, overhangs must be kept to a minimum so that good acoustic conditions are maintained beneath the overhang. Fig. 6.11 illustrates the permissible depth of overhang for acoustic reasons, whereby the overhung depth should not exceed the height from the ground floor to the balcony soffit.

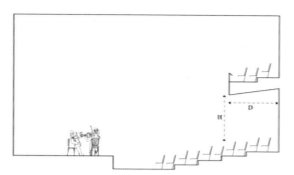

Fig. 6.11 Recommended balcony overhang dimensions: the depth D should not exceed the height H.

An alternative to the rectangular plan shape is the elongated hexagon, as shown in Fig. 6.12 below. This shape can also provide good visual and acoustic intimacy.

In terms of ceiling shape, a flat ceiling with some surface modelling is appropriate; a steeply pitched ceiling (around 45 degrees) is also good. Shallow pitches of around 10 degrees or less should be avoided because they can cause disturbing repetitive reflections between the flat floor and the ceiling.

Shapes with concave surfaces such as domes and barrel vaults are best avoided because they cause focusing of sound, which can result in problematic acoustics. Where concave surfaces are unavoidable and cause a focus near the audience or performance area, heavily absorbing or diffusing elements should be deployed. There are circumstances where focusing can provide a useful acoustical benefit, such as enhancing the sound in certain seating areas; however, this approach could be dangerous in practice, and should only be undertaken following detailed acoustic analysis.

Surface finishes are generally hard and acoustically reflective – for example a timber floor, brickwork walls and a timber ceiling. Almost all the acoustic absorption is provided by the audience and seating.

Where there is no fixed seating or retractable (bleacher) seating, movable acoustic drapes can be provided on the rear and side walls. These can be extended to control reverberation in rehearsal conditions when the seats are removed. Drapes will also provide suitable conditions when amplified music is being played, and also for spoken word performances.

A seating rake is beneficial because it provides better sightlines, and this also improves the acoustic quality for listeners. A rake of 8 degrees is suitable, but a much steeper rake should be avoided because musicians and singers find it difficult performing into a highly absorbent surface: it reduces the valuable feedback they get from the hall.

It is often required to arrange performances in a hall in various configurations, and this can be achieved by providing some flexibility in the design; this usually involves installing retractable seating. An example of how this can be achieved is illustrated in the diagrams in Fig. 6.13.

Recital Halls with a Pitched Ceiling

The shape of a music auditorium will inevitably have an influence over the sequence of reflections arriving at a listener; many recital halls that are based on the 'shoebox' plan tend to be divided between those with a pitched ceiling and those with a flat ceiling. There doesn't appear to be any difference in the sound quality between the two shapes, and both types can be very successful. Examples are given below of the two types.

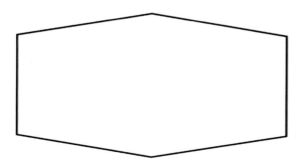

Fig. 6.12 Plan of an elongated hexagon, an alternative to the rectangular plan.

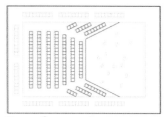

Drama performance on stage

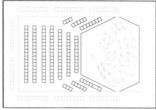

Orchestra performance on stage

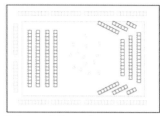

Performance in the round

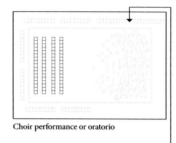

Choir performance or oratorio

Balcony above

Fig. 6.13 Various
configurations
of a hall for
performing arts.

The Precedent of Snape Maltings Concert Hall

The 800-seat concert hall at Snape Maltings, created for the composer Benjamin Britten to provide a suitable venue for his Aldeburgh Festival, was formed by restructuring a disused Victorian maltings building; it was completed in 1970. To ensure sufficient acoustic volume, the design involved raising the height of the walls by 1m (3ft) and installing a new pitched roof with a pitch angle of 45 degrees. The design was developed by Arup Associates, led by their eminent acoustician, Derek Sugden. A view of the completed hall is shown in Fig. 6.14.

Fig. 6.14 Snape Maltings Concert Hall. (Courtesy Arup)

The quality of the sound in the hall was soon recognized, and Snape Maltings concert hall has developed a reputation for having one of the best acoustics in the UK. Owing to its success, the design of the Snape concert hall has influenced the design of numerous recital halls designed and built subsequently. Examples are described in the following section.

Edward Boyle Auditorium in the Jaqueline du Pré Music Building

The Jacqueline du Pré Music Building at St Hilda's College, Oxford, was designed to provide facilities for the performance and practice of music. It contains the Edward Boyle auditorium, a 200-seat recital hall, and a number of large and small practice rooms. The design was developed by van Heyningen and Haward Architects, with acoustics by Arup; the influence of

Derek Sugden and the Snape Maltings concert hall is clearly in evidence.

The shape is rectangular in plan, with a pitched ceiling at a pitch angle of 45 degrees (*see* plan and section in Fig. 6.15). It has a volume per seat of $6m^3$ ($7yd^3$), which resulted in a reverberation time of 1.3 seconds when it is occupied. The narrow plan provides strong early reflections from the sidewalls, together with cue-ball reflections from these walls via the balcony soffits, which help to achieve a good balance between clarity and reverberance. A view of the auditorium is shown in Fig. 6.16.

Surface finishes are masonry and timber, which are hard and acoustically reflective in order to maintain reverberation and to enhance it at low frequencies to give 'warmth' to the sound. The engineering of the ceiling is particularly interesting in this respect as it comprises a 150mm (6in) thick layer

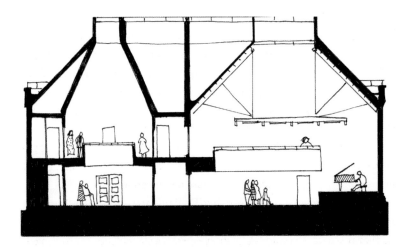

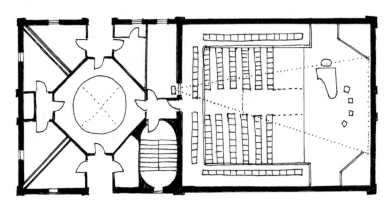

Fig. 6.15 Plan and section of the Edward Boyle auditorium in the Jaqueline du Pré Music Building. (Courtesy van Heyningen and Haward Architects)

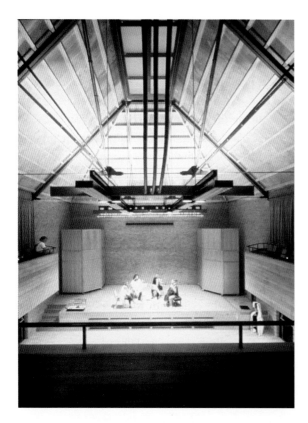

Fig. 6.16 The Edward Boyle auditorium in the Jaqueline du Pré Music Building. (Photo: Charlotte Wood)

To provide a very quiet background, necessary for hearing the full dynamic range of the music, the walls are constructed of heavy masonry, and the roof is formed using sprayed concrete, as mentioned above. Noise from the mechanical ventilation system is silenced to virtual inaudibility.

The Jacqueline du Pré Music Building has now been in successful operation for over twenty-five years. As well as providing facilities for music students of the college, it hosts concerts by international musicians; the eminent cellist Stephen Isserlis acts as patron.

Pamoja Concert Hall and Recital Hall at Sevenoaks School

A new performing arts centre was built at Sevenoaks School and completed in 2010; its centrepiece is the Pamoja Hall, a 450-seat concert hall with a stage large enough to take a symphony orchestra. The building also includes a recital hall capable of accommodating 100 people, a drama studio, and twenty-four music and drama teaching spaces. The architect was Tim Ronalds Architects, with acoustics by Arup.

The Pamoja Hall was designed to accommodate two main functions – namely, music and assembly, which, of course, require two different types of acoustic. The approach was to design the hall for music and to make it adaptable for the spoken word.

There were two fundamental options for the shape of the hall: a traditional shoebox with a flat ceiling, or a traditional shoebox with a steeply pitched roof, such as at the Snape Maltings concert hall. The latter option was chosen, partly because it would provide the large acoustic volume required (4,700m³/5,620yd³), and partly because it avoided a large, box-like form on the site.

The plan shape is basically rectangular – 18m (59ft) wide × 25m (82ft) long – and the roof pitch is 50 degrees. The main body of the seating is raked, and this is surrounded by a balcony, with one row of seats that runs all round the hall. Good sightlines are available from all seats. The surface finishes, apart

of concrete, lined internally with plywood, to keep out external noise. To ensure that the concrete was in direct contact with the plywood to eliminate the possibility of panel absorption at low frequencies, dry concrete (Gunite) was sprayed on to a double layer of plywood, which acted as permanent shuttering. The advantage of the Gunite is that it sticks fast to whatever it is sprayed on to. The result is a very solid ceiling with virtually no absorption at low frequencies.

Variability of the acoustics can be obtained by drawing acoustic curtains over the walls at the rear and sides of the gallery, which, when fully extended, reduce the reverberation time to 1 second, which is suitable for the spoken word. At the other extreme, the curtains can be bunched and all the seats stacked at the rear, which results in a reverberation time of 2 seconds, which is suitable for recording sessions.

from the seating, are hard and acoustically reflective, and comprise natural materials such as timber and brick. Surface diffusion is modest and is provided largely by structural elements including rafters, columns and ceiling battens. (A view of the hall is shown in Fig. 6.17.)

A special feature of the hall is that it is naturally ventilated despite the site being on the flight path to Gatwick airport. The air supply is via an acoustically lined labyrinth that leads to a plenum under the seating rake with outlets under the seats. 18m (59ft) above floor level the exhaust air passes via a vent into a giant linear acoustic silencer fitted with acoustic linings and baffles, and then leaves through a ridge cowl with top-hung flaps on the down-wind side. The target internal noise level was extremely low (NR20), and this has been met without difficulty.

When the concert hall is used for assemblies where speech intelligibility is the key factor, acoustic banners are dropped down from banner boxes in the ceiling. The banner mechanisms are motorized, and this system provides a simple and effective way of reducing the reverberant sound.

The adjacent recital hall, which caters for smaller, more intimate performances, is approximately rectangular in plan, but none of the walls is parallel. The roof is pitched and forms an asymmetric pyramid surmounting the walls. This asymmetry promotes sound diffusion in what would otherwise be a box-shaped room with large areas of glazing, which could have been susceptible to flutter echoes and prominent standing waves. Additional small-scale diffusion is provided by battens on the ceiling and timber ribs on the walls. The acoustic can be varied by movable drapes that run around the walls. A view of the hall is shown in Fig. 6.18.

Fig. 6.17 Pamoja Hall at Sevenoaks School. (Courtesy Tim Ronalds Architects. Photo: © Christian Richters/VIEW)

Fig. 6.18 The Recital Hall at Sevenoaks School. (Courtesy Tim Ronalds Architects. Photo: © Christian Richters/VIEW)

The Britten Studio at Snape Maltings

When it came to the design of a recital hall for Aldeburgh Music at Snape Maltings, the issue of acoustics was of paramount importance, and the very high standards set by the Snape Maltings Concert Hall had to be maintained. The same questions that the concert hall's original acoustician, Derek Sugden, had addressed some forty years earlier on roof shape and volume were considered again by the design team, which was led by architects Haworth Tompkins with acoustics by Arup. Several options were mooted, but the answers remained unchanged: namely a pitched roof and ample volume.

The new hall, named the Britten Studio, is a smaller space than the concert hall and accommodates mainly orchestral rehearsals and recitals, although it is also used for the spoken word. In broad terms, the Britten Studio has slightly less than half the seating capacity of the main hall: the number of seats is 350, and it is around half the volume. It is rectangular in plan, with raked seating. The construction of the auditorium envelope, including the roof, is of concrete to ensure a very low internal background so the full dynamic range of the music can be appreciated. A view of the hall is shown in Fig. 6.19.

Fig. 6.19 The Britten Studio at Snape Maltings. (Courtesy Howard Tompkins Architects. Photo: Philip Vile)

Fig. 6.20 The Britten Studio showing the modulated walls at low level, and the timber panels at high level. (Courtesy Howard Tompkins Architects. Photo: Philip Vile)

Internally, the upper part of the concrete walls is clad with timber panels: this provides a mixture of sound-absorbing, reflecting and diffusing surfaces, giving a well-balanced acoustic response across the whole sound spectrum. Where the concrete walls are left exposed at low level they form convex modulations to diffuse the sound, giving a uniform distribution over the stage and seating areas. A particular feature of these concrete areas is that the concrete has been washed back whilst drying to expose the stone aggregate below; this provides small-scale convex protrusions, which diffuse sound at high frequencies. These concrete walls therefore provide sound diffusion at both low and high frequencies (the wall construction is shown in Fig. 6.20).

But the new hall is not just a chip off the old block. To enable orchestral rehearsal, the seats can be fully retracted to provide a large, flat floor where the orchestra can spread itself out. In this mode, where there is no audience, the sound has to be controlled, otherwise it would get too loud with full orchestral forces. This control is provided by dropping down acoustic banners within the ceiling zone, together with deploying acoustic drapes on the end walls. This acoustic variability permits many other types of activity to take place, such as opera rehearsal, chamber opera performances, masterclasses and other public events.

The Hoffmann building (its exterior appearance is shown in Fig. 6.21), which contains the Britten Studio, also contains a smaller music space called the Jerwood Kiln Studio, which is built within a former kiln. The same acoustic design philosophy has been used in this space, with ample acoustic volume being provided by the original steeply sloped ceiling (*see* Fig. 6.22).

Fig. 6.21 The Hoffmann Building with the Snape Maltings Concert Hall in the background. (Courtesy Howard Tompkins Architects. Photo: Philip Vile)

Fig. 6.22 The Kiln Studio in the Hoffman building at Snape Maltings. (Courtesy Howard Tompkins Architects. Photo: Philip Vile)

The Recital Hall at the Merritt Centre at Sherborne Girls School

The new recital hall at Sherborne Girls School, which was completed in 2019, has also adopted the shape of the Snape Maltings Concert Hall in order to provide the acoustic advantages of the 'shoebox' geometry and to ensure a generous volume resulting from the pitched roof. The architects were Burrell Foley Fischer, with acoustic advice by Ramboll.

The main difference of this particular design is that the whole building, including the adjacent music practice rooms and foyer, was constructed of cross-laminated timber (CLT). This material has the advantage that considerable parts of the construction can be carried out efficiently off site, and consequently the erection time on site is much shorter. An acoustical disadvantage of CLT is that it is considerably less dense than masonry, and therefore provides less sound insulation. Therefore care had to be taken

to ensure that wall and roof build-ups were heavy enough to provide sufficient sound insulation; for example, the roof consisted of multiple boards, one of which was a heavy cementitious board.

The brief for the hall was to provide a recital space that could accommodate a full orchestra and 300 audience seats. In addition the hall was to be used for assemblies for 560 students, who could be accommodated by retracting the seating. Variable acoustics were to be included so the acoustics between music and speech could be adjusted.

The shape of the auditorium readily provides all the key room acoustic requirements; the volume is around 4,000m^3 (4,785yd^3), which ensures ample reverberation and also controls loudness. The narrow plan shape provides strong early reflections, giving clarity to the sound; many of these early reflections are from a lateral direction, which provides a desirable sense of spaciousness or 'surround sound'. A view of the hall is shown in Fig. 6.23.

Fig. 6.23 The recital hall in the Merritt Centre at Sherborne Girls School.

To ensure that the sidewall reflections are controlled in strength and distributed evenly over the seating area, a degree of diffusion is added to the wall surfaces by lining them with timber battens of different depths; the same treatment is applied to the wall behind the performers. A detail of the timber battening is shown in Fig. 6.24.

The variable acoustics are provided by banners, which drop down from the eaves along the upper parts of the sidewalls; the area of the banners when

Fig. 6.24 Sound diffusion produced by timber battening of varying depths.

fully extended is 200m² (240yd²). They are motorized, and can be deployed within a minute or so, and fit neatly within a step from the lower part of the sidewalls.

The acoustic outcome of the completed hall satisfies the brief very well; the measured reverberation time (when it is unoccupied) for recitals is 1.5 seconds, which is close to ideal, and with the banners deployed it is 1.1 seconds, which is good for speech. When the seats are retracted, the reverberation time increases to 1.8 seconds, which is suitable for orchestral rehearsal.

Recital Halls with a Flat Ceiling

The Clarendon Muse, Watford

The Clarendon Muse is a recital hall within a new music school that includes twenty-one music practice rooms, classrooms and a recording facility. It was a joint venture between Watford Grammar School and Watford School of Music; it was designed by Tim Ronalds Architects, and completed in 2007, with acoustics by Arup. The brief for the recital hall was to support teaching, and performances ranging from solo instrumentalists to full orchestras in both the classical and contemporary musical genres.

The whole building has a simple rectilinear shape with a flat roof, and sits well on the sloping site (*see* the outside view in Fig. 6.25); the external cladding comprises opaque glass and aluminium, which has given rise to the building's nickname: 'the ice cube'. The hall follows the same rectilinear shape with a flat ceiling, and provides a large rectangular performance area, with the audience, numbering 200, arranged on raked seating to provide good sightlines and 'sound-lines' and a sense of intimacy. The volume of the hall is ample to provide sufficient reverberation with the flexibility of softening the sound of a full orchestra or other loud ensembles such as brass bands by deploying floor-to-ceiling drapes.

Fig. 6.25 Exterior view of Clarendon Muse.

Fig. 6.26 The recital hall at Clarendon Muse.

The internal finish on both walls and ceiling is a multiple-layered heavy plasterboard lining to maintain a strong bass response. This lining is subtly modulated in a zig-zag pattern to diffuse incident sound in order to give a uniform distribution of reflections throughout the space. The zig-zag modelling is not particularly noticeable on the walls, but forms interesting forms on the ceiling. The floor is timber-bonded to masonry to further support the bass.

The external envelope is of concrete to keep out the noise of the nearby road, which carries heavy traffic. The generously sized windows including a roof-light are acoustically double glazed for the same reason. The ventilation system has also been designed to achieve a very low background noise so that musical performances can achieve beautiful pianissimo when required. A view of the performance area is shown in Fig. 6.26.

The Clarendon Muse has proved very successful both for teaching and as a national performance venue for the wider community. It has been included as an exemplar in the Department for Education design guide 'Music accommodation in secondary schools'.

Cosmo Rodewald Concert Hall, Manchester

The Cosmo Rodewald Concert Hall is the main music performance space at the Martin Harris Centre for Music and Drama at the University of Manchester. It hosts an extensive series of professional concerts and recitals, including major series by resident string quartets. The venue has 350 seats and a spacious stage large enough to accommodate a full symphony orchestra (Fig. 6.27). A particularly interesting feature of the design is the ceiling: this comprises a large, flat array of panels that are trapezoidal in shape and gently convex when viewed from underneath.

The panels alternate in their orientation, and there are gaps between them which connect the acoustic volume below the panels to the volume in the void above; this void contains the roof structure and elements of the building services. This connection between the two volumes is essential to ensure that there is sufficient overall volume to provide ample reverberance; therefore around 20 per cent of the ceiling is open to ensure acoustic coupling between the two volumes. The panels are made from glass-reinforced gypsum (GRG), which is hard and acoustically reflective, providing an even coverage of sound over the seating area.

To provide a degree of diffusion on the surfaces around the performers to help them hear each other clearly, vertical timber battens have been fixed to the walls in a pseudo-random arrangement. These battens are sparser on the sidewalls and then become more concentrated on the rear wall to avoid a delayed reflection from there back to the stage.

Fig. 6.27 Cosmo Rodewald Concert Hall, Manchester University. (Courtesy Martin Harris Centre)

The Stoller Concert Hall, Manchester

The Stoller Hall is the main performance space at Chetham's School of Music; it is contained within a new teaching building. The construction of this new building went ahead as planned, but the design of the hall was delayed to enable funds to be raised – a space was left in the shell of the building to accommodate the hall. Fortunately, a major donation by Sir Norman Stoller, together with additional donations, enabled the construction to proceed within five years of the initial conception.

Stoller Hall was designed by architect Roger Stephenson with acoustics by Arup, it has 480 seats and is used predominantly for recitals, chamber music and recording. The design has incorporated a variable acoustic system using drop-down banners which shortens the reverberation time and renders the space suitable for amplified performances and also for conferences.

The hall is located in the lower part of the building, partly below ground, so that a rectilinear shape with a flat ceiling was the clear choice (Fig. 6.28). It is not a perfect shoebox but rather it is gently lozenge shaped where the walls at both front and rear are angled in slightly. This provides a natural enclosure for the stage; at the rear, the slight angling makes sidewall reflections more lateral. To minimize noise intrusion from adjacent musical activities and to avoid residual noise from nearby trains, the hall is built of heavy masonry and structurally isolated from the rest of the building by supporting it on resilient bearings.

Fig. 6.28 The Stoller Concert Hall, Chetham's School of Music: view towards the stage. (Photo courtesy of Arup)

To optimize the room acoustics, the walls at low level are made from oak panels that are stepped in and out to provide sound diffusion at high frequencies. At high level, the walls are also modulated but provide diffusion at low frequencies. The ceiling includes lightweight panelling that absorbs low frequency sound to a certain extent by the mechanism of panel absorption; this prevents the hall from sounding 'boomy'.

The Stoller Hall incorporates all the latest thinking in the acoustic design of recital halls, particularly in terms of shape, sound diffusion and sound absorption.

Recital Halls with Concave Geometries

Edwina Palmer Hall, Benslow Music

Benslow Music is a ninety-year-old organization that runs residential courses for musicians. It is based on a small campus near Hitchin, Hertfordshire, which was expanded in 2000 by the addition of a second recital hall, practice rooms and an accommodation block. The architects, Patel Taylor, opted for an asymmetrical plan shape featuring a large concave wall with a roof formed by an asymmetric cone (Fig. 6.29).

The proposed concave geometry of the curved wall would undoubtedly have caused serious focusing of sound. A group of players near such a focus would each hear differences in loudness, which would make playing in good ensemble difficult. Similar undesirable variations in loudness would occur in the audience. To counteract this focusing, the conventional approach is to break up the concave geometry with stepped surfaces or convex shapes to provide a degree of sound diffusion. The results are not always satisfactory architecturally.

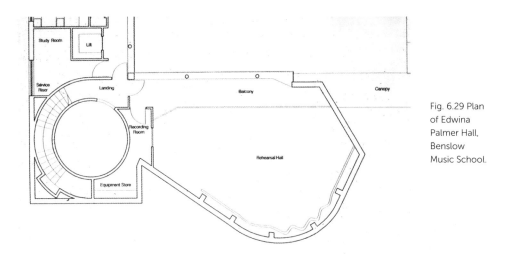

Fig. 6.29 Plan of Edwina Palmer Hall, Benslow Music School.

Research by Professor Trevor Cox at Salford University and his colleague Peter D'Antonio has led to the possibility of generating surface geometries mathematically, which will provide the exact degree of sound diffusion required (Cox and D'Antonio 2004). What is particularly attractive about this technique is that a 'shape motif' can be chosen by the designers, which can be a continuous wave, a stepped surface or some other preferred geometrical form. This shape is then optimized, or morphed, by the mathematical process to give the precise diffusing surface.

The technique to optimize shape was applied to the design of the Edwina Palmer recital hall, where it was decided that maximum diffusion was required because of the severity of the curvature of the wall. The architects chose a continuous sinusoidal shape for the final geometric form of the wall. The output of the mathematical modelling resulted in a skewed sinusoidal curve of varying amplitude, which follows the curve of the original wall (Fig. 6.30).

The optimized 'wiggly' wall satisfied the architects' design intentions and met the acoustical requirements to neutralize the focusing. The wall, shown in Fig. 6.31, was formed from 25mm-thick medium-density fibreboard (MDF) with a paint finish. To enhance the appearance of the wall, the architects added thin vertical strips to the curves, and stepped the wall back at high level; these add-ons did not significantly affect the sound-diffusing properties.

Fig. 6.30 Optimized profile for diffusing incident sound.

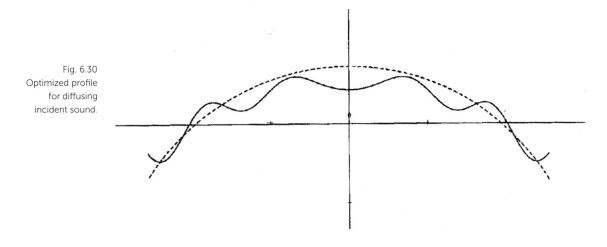

Fig. 6.31 The Edwina Palmer Hall, Benslow Music School.

With regard to the asymmetrical conical ceiling, there was also concern about focusing from this geometry. This was addressed by designing the ceiling as a series of pseudo-random steps, providing sound diffusion over a range of frequencies.

In reviewing the recital hall, the *Architectural Review* (May 2002) referred to the shaped wall as 'free-form wooden screening', which lends 'a sculptural dimension to the space'. The beauty of this approach is that it enables the combination of precise acoustical performance with the desired architectural form.

The Wigmore Hall, London

The Wigmore Hall in London, formerly known as Bechstein Hall, was designed by the Victorian architect Thomas Collcutt; it held its inaugural concert in 1901. Until World War I it was used as a showroom for the German piano manufacturer, Bechstein, and from 1917 onwards it has been open to the public as a recital hall specializing in chamber music. A view of the hall is shown in Fig. 6.32. The Hall has acquired an outstanding reputation as one of the leading venues in Europe for chamber music and its acoustics are considered by both audience and performers to be second to none.

The characteristic qualities of the sound in the hall are described as loud, spacious, intimate, moderately reverberant yet clear. The sound in the balcony is particularly favoured by some. The acoustic is most suited to small chamber ensembles such as string quartets and solo instrumental recitals. For ensembles of more than, say, eight musicians, the stage is too small.

What is remarkable about the Wigmore Hall is the relationship between the excellence of its acoustics and certain anomalies of its geometric shape. The first anomaly is that the volume of the hall, which is $2,900m^3$ ($3,470yd^3$), appears rather small for the number of seats, namely 544. This gives a volume per seat of $5.3m^3$ ($6.3yd^3$), which would be expected to give a reverberation time close to 1 second – and yet the reverberation time when the hall is occupied is 1.5 seconds an ideal value for a recital hall.

Fig. 6.32 The Wigmore Hall.

There are three other major anomalies: the elliptical barrel vault ceiling, the cylindrical apse at the rear of the stage, and the cupola that surmounts it. The remaining aspects of the hall are more conventional, as it is rectangular on plan (12.3 × 22.9m (40 × 75ft)), and the seats are arranged mainly on the flat floor with the rest on a small balcony at the rear.

The presence of large areas of concave surfaces introduces a high risk of focusing, which is liable to cause acoustical faults such as an uneven distribution of sound over both stage and audience, flutter echoes, and unusually strong reflections causing possible image shifting. Yet these faults are not apparent in the hall, and the focusing may actually be benign or even beneficial.

An opportunity to investigate the focusing effects in the hall presented itself when the hall underwent a major refurbishment in 2003/4; this involved replacement of the seats and carpet, introducing a very quiet ventilation system, and improving the sound insulation of the roof (Wulfrank 2006).

When investigating reflections from curved surfaces, it is important to remember that the reflected sound, under certain conditions, can be diffused rather than focused. These conditions are governed by the geometric relationship between the sound source, the receiver and the reflective surface.

The ceiling of the Wigmore Hall is hemi-elliptical in cross-section, which causes two foci; however, they occur well above the musicians and the audience and therefore do not pose any acoustic problems. However, focusing still causes significant amplification of sound in the stalls, which is caused by reflections from the central part of the ceiling. By contrast, reflections from the extremes of the curved ceiling are diffused rather than focused.

In the balcony, amplification also occurs, but this is dominated by areas of the ceiling either side of the central zone. This means that these reflections are

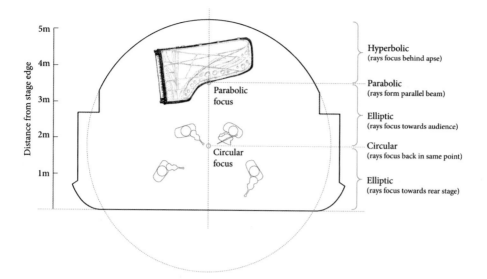

Fig. 6.33 Plan of the stage at Wigmore Hall (after Wulfrank).

The labels in the figure from top to bottom on the right:

Hyperbolic (rays focus behind apse)

Parabolic (rays form parallel beam)

Elliptic (rays focus towards audience)

Circular (rays focus back in same point)

Elliptic (rays focus towards rear stage)

Labels within the plan: Parabolic focus, Circular focus

Y-axis: Distance from stage edge — 5m, 4m, 3m, 2m, 1m

more lateral than in the stalls, and possibly increase not only the loudness but the sense of spaciousness in the balcony. Subjectively, regular concert goers and discerning listeners have noted that the sound in the balcony has ample loudness and a sense of spaciousness.

The stage of the Wigmore Hall is dominated at its rear by an apse, which in plan is the section of a circle with a radius of around 3.5m (11.5ft) (*see* Fig. 6.33). This surface causes some amplification in the audience area, but the strength depends on the location of the sound source on stage, whether front, centre or rear. For a sound source at the front of the stage, there is virtually no amplification for the audience, but this increases moderately as the source position moves further upstage.

In addition to the amplification effects, the apse produces some acoustic peculiarities, which could be considered acoustic faults. For example, for a listener towards the rear of the stalls, the cello and the second violin in a string quartet can be perceived as reversed. Thus, the sound of the cello appears to be coming from the left whereas the second violin can be heard as coming from the right.

Another peculiarity is the existence on stage of reasonably strong and late reflections (delayed by 160ms) near the focus of the apse. This happens because the apse reflects sound from this point as a beam of parallel rays, which remain parallel when travelling back after reflection off the rear wall, and which re-converge at the focus. However, this does not seem to disturb the performers, but rather gives them useful musical support.

The cupola surmounting the stage apse is a quarter sphere with a radius of curvature of 3.5m (11.5ft). Its geometrical coverage for first order reflections from typical stage sources extends over most of the audience area, including the balcony. However, contrary to what might be expected, no focusing occurs from the cupola – rather, it acts as a diffuser. This diffusing property is likely to be beneficial, as it reduces the risk of false localization.

Summarizing the acoustic peculiarities of the Wigmore Hall caused by the curved surfaces, they appear to be causing beneficial focusing together with a modest degree of diffusion, which creates a very favourable sound for chamber music. This effect is very complex, as suggested in the above analysis, and has been arrived at by probably a mixture of good chance and precedent. It would be very risky to attempt a similar design with such large areas of curved surface without very detailed analysis using both computer and scale models.

Chapter Seven

Other Building Types

Worship Spaces

As far back as the Stone Age, people explored caves to find spaces that were reverberant, and when they found them they painted pictures on the walls and are likely to have enacted rituals. Even an outdoor enclosure such as Stonehenge may have included special sounds during rituals, and this has recently been the subject of an acoustic study. The results show that the original henge did, in fact, create a degree of reverberation that would have reinforced musical sounds performed within the central circle (Cox 2010).

However, it is interesting to jump forward to the Christian era, and particularly the Renaissance period, where there was a flourishing of spectacular church building in such places as Venice. The question that arises is this: 'Did the architects at that time have an understanding of acoustics, and did they develop their designs with acoustics in mind?'

Acoustics in Churches of the Renaissance, Particularly Venice

Venice was one of the centres of the flowering of art and architecture in the Renaissance period, and some of the most eminent architects of the period designed and built churches there. Probably the most famous is Andrea Palladio, who is widely considered to be one of the most influential architects in the history of architecture. His compatriot, Jacopo Sansovino, is also highly respected, and was responsible for a number of important Venetian churches.

Palladio was influenced by the Roman architect Vitruvius, who, as mentioned in the first chapter, had an understanding of acoustics and its importance in architectural design. For example, Vitruvius said that cornices are important for reflecting sound back into the interior. Although Renaissance architects were familiar with Vitruvius' ideas, they actively discussed various ceiling types; some considered vaulted ceilings were difficult for speech, saying that they cause too much resonance. Some suggested that flat wooden ceilings with beams give a better sound – for example, the Franciscan friar and learned humanist, Francesco Zorzi, wrote in 1535 that they would improve the audibility of sermons. Another idea of the time was that relief is important, and that smooth surfaces of a dome cause too much reverberation. Yet another idea was that niches in music rooms improved the quality of sound by interrupting reflections.

It is interesting to note that some of these ideas have a strong correlation with current auditorium design.

To answer the question of how far did architects consider acoustics in church design, an extensive research study was carried out on twelve Venetian churches of the Renaissance period, including ones by Palladio and Sansovino (Howard & Moretti 2009). The study involved careful listening to an experienced choir (St John's College, Cambridge) singing music of the period in all the churches, coupled with acoustic measurements of reverberation time and other key acoustical parameters.

The results of the study indicated that churches designed by Sansovino had, or intended to have, flat timber ceilings in the nave – this aligns with Zorzi's advice that such ceilings are good for speech. Also, there is a strong suggestion that Sansovino worked with the composer Adriano Willaert, who was also the choirmaster at the Basilica di San Marco, to install two choir balconies in the chancel to provide excellent listening conditions for the Doge of Venice and his entourage. A view towards the chancel of the Basilica di San Marco is shown in Fig. 7.1, and a view of the choir balconies inside the chancel is shown in Fig. 7.2.

In the case of Palladio, it remains difficult to answer the question. His two main churches, San Giorgio Maggiore and the Redentore (Fig. 7.3) are very reverberant and not suited to music, particularly the complex music developed in the Renaissance.

The overall conclusion is that the design of churches in the Renaissance period paid some attention to acoustics, particularly in seating areas for influential worshippers, and it appears that some architects, such as Sansovino, took into account the knowledge that was then available.

Fig. 7.2 The choir balconies in the chancel of the Basilica di San Marco.

Fig. 7.3 Interior of the Redentore by architect Andrea Palladio.

The Acoustic Importance of the Pulpit and its Sounding Board

The Venetian friar, Francesco Zorzi, who advised on one of Sansovino's churches, San Francesco della Vigna, had the right idea when he suggested that a flat

Fig. 7.1 View towards the chancel of the Basilica di San Marco.

wooden ceiling would improve speech intelligibility; however, he did not specify the height of the ceiling above the speaker, which is a crucial dimension for providing a strong early reflection.

It was clearly becoming a problem in the sixteenth century, and probably earlier, that the reverberation in churches was too long to enable intelligible speech. To help overcome the excessive reverberation, the speaker was lifted above the congregation on to a pulpit; this increased the strength of the direct sound from speaker to listener. This is because when a speaker is at the same level as the listeners, the sound passes over the listeners' heads at grazing incidence, and this results in a more rapid loss of sound energy than in the free field.

Raising the speaker on to a pulpit was probably not enough in reverberant churches to provide reliably intelligible speech. In fundamental terms, it is necessary to increase the early reflections that enhance speech, and to decrease the reverberation that degrades it. This was neatly resolved by placing a sounding board above the pulpit not far above the speaker's head (Fig. 7.4). This produces a strong early reflection and directs it to the congregation. In addition, it reduces the amount of sound energy going upwards, which would become reverberant energy; thus this simple device substantially improved speech intelligibility in reverberant churches.

Sometimes the sounding boards were dished and angled to provide a more focused sound on to the congregation: this increased the ratio of early to reverberant sound even more.

Electroacoustics Supersede the Role of the Sounding Board

Most parish churches and cathedrals built in England before the twentieth century were constructed of stone with large volumes, which resulted in long reverberation times. For example, the reverberation time in St Paul's Cathedral is 11 seconds when empty

Fig. 7.4 A sounding board above a raised pulpit.

and 7.8 seconds when full. Elevating the speaker on to a pulpit with a sounding board overhead certainly helped speech intelligibility, but the advent of electroacoustics in the twentieth century resulted in a major step forwards.

The key to successful speech reinforcement in churches was the design of the loudspeakers. In essence, loudspeakers were required that would beam the sound towards the congregation and avoid spreading it out in other directions, in a similar way to the sounding board. This led to the development of the column loudspeaker, which is basically a vertical array of loudspeakers in a cabinet; an acoustical interference effect occurs between the loudspeakers, which concentrates the sound into a beam, which is narrow in the vertical plane but remains the same in the horizontal plane.

The sharpness of the beam depends on the length of the column and the frequency of the sound. Column loudspeakers developed in the 1950s for installation in cathedrals such as St Paul's and Salisbury were typically 3.3m (10.8ft) long (Fig. 7.5); they were mounted slightly above ear height and tilted forwards towards the congregation.

A single column at the front of a large church was not enough to cover the whole congregation, and so additional columns were positioned along the nave. This presented the problem that sound from a column that was distant from the actual speaker would arrive at a listener before the speaker's voice itself, which feels unnatural. To resolve this problem, time delays were added to the more distant loudspeakers so that the natural voice arrived first and was followed by the loudspeaker sound. The use of time delays enabled a particular effect of the hearing system, known as the Haas effect, to be used advantageously. This effect enables a sound, which is delayed from the original sound by up to 25ms, to be almost twice as loud as the original sound but not perceivable as a separate source. Thus the sound from the loudspeakers could be substantially louder than the actual speaker but the sound would appear as coming from the speaker and would sound natural.

Fig. 7.5 A column loudspeaker from the 1950s.

Modern sound reinforcement systems still use long column loudspeakers, although they are slimmer and technically much more sophisticated; they can be mounted vertically with the beam direction adjusted electronically.

Principles of Worship Space Design

Both speech and music typically take place in worship spaces, and it is important at the outset of design to determine the importance of speech intelligibility in the services and the type of music being performed; it is also necessary to ascertain the architectural aspirations, particularly in terms of volume, which tends to be large because of the desire for height.

In cathedrals and large parish churches, there will usually be organ music, choral singing and congregational singing, which will require a reasonably long reverberation time of, say, 3 seconds. This length of reverberation time aligns well with the usual architectural requirement of a generous volume and hard surfaces. Speech intelligibility will also be very important, but rather than having a short reverberation time, good speech intelligibility is achieved by a custom-designed speech-reinforcement system as described above. The principle of the design is therefore to provide appropriate acoustics for music, and to use a speech-reinforcement system for speech.

The placement of the choir and organ is important for achieving a good musical result. The organ, organ console and singers should ideally be within a 10m (33ft) radius to avoid acoustical time-delay problems. The choirmaster must hear the organ without excessive delay, and must also be close enough to hear the choir without significant delay.

Good locations for the choir are behind the altar or the upstage chancel wall, facing the congregation, and preferably elevated above it. An alternative location is a reasonably high rear balcony or gallery. In either case, the organ and choir should face down the main axis of the church. It is useful to have sound-reflecting surfaces near the choir to enable them to hear themselves well.

Another type of church service is where the music is amplified and a leader leads the whole congregation in lively singing, as typified by gospel music. This type of church requires a short reverberation time in the range 1–1.5 seconds, which will require a significant amount of sound absorption on the walls and ceiling, depending on the volume. The loudspeakers for both speech and music should be directed towards the congregation as in other sound-reinforcement systems.

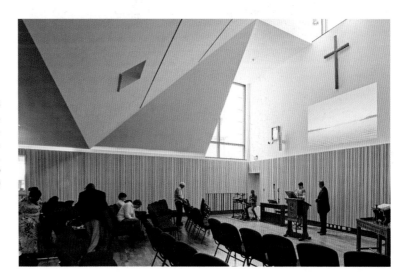

Fig. 7.6 Crossways Church, Southwark, London. (Architects: vHH. Photo: Carlo Draisi)

An example of a small twenty-first-century church where this type of music takes place is the Crossways Church in Southwark, London, by architects vHH with acoustics by Ramboll (Fig. 7.6). The acoustical design of the worship space is aimed at reproducing the amplified sound as faithfully as possible without coloration (like a sound studio), whilst having sufficient reverberation to enable the singing of the congregation to bloom. To achieve this, the walls at low level are clad in timber slats, with sections of the slats backed by sound absorption: this produces a partly sound-absorbing and partly sound-diffusing surface. The loudspeaker sound is directed towards these low-level surfaces so that strong reflections and coloration are avoided. The walls at high level, above the celebrants' area, rise up to two storeys and form a chamber-like space where the singing can reverberate.

Not all worship spaces have music and singing; certain religions, such as Islam, only recite prayers in their special prayer venues, namely mosques. The design of mosques can be challenging as they tend to have large volumes and therefore long reverberation times, and often include a dome that will focus sound; yet they are only required for speech, which requires a short reverberation time.

It is interesting to look at the design of a twenty-first-century mosque completed in 2019 in Cambridge, UK, by architects Marks Barfield, with acoustics by Ramboll (Fig. 7.7).

The prayer room inside the mosque can accommodate up to 1,000 worshippers and certainly has a large volume. The reverberation time is controlled by having a carpeted floor, and also helpful is the diffusion provided by the intricate timber columns. The measured reverberation time when the mosque

Fig. 7.7 The prayer room at the Cambridge mosque. (Architects: Marks Barfield)

is empty is 2 seconds; this may appear long for a space used only for speech, but the space has a calm atmosphere and the speech of the Imam is reinforced by a high quality sound-reinforcement system.

The worship space does have a dome in the centre, but it has a relatively small diameter so the focus is high above the worshippers and does not produce a focusing problem.

The Cambridge mosque is proving to be a fine example of a twenty-first-century worship space, which works well acoustically.

Law Courts

The criminal justice system depends primarily on the spoken word, and so it is of paramount importance that speech intelligibility is very good for all users in the courtroom. In addition, extraneous noise from external sources or from the building services systems should be reduced to a minimum to avoid disturbance and distraction.

The reverberation time in a courtroom should be around 1 second or thereabouts; this will provide good conditions for natural speech, and it will also enable the speech-reinforcement system to work effectively. Consideration must be given to those with hearing impairment, which could include a judge, a juror or a defendant. Although hearing impairment is aided by an electronic loop system, good room acoustics will help in maximizing intelligibility.

In the court building as a whole it is particularly important to control the transmission of sound between various key spaces, such as interview rooms, to provide an appropriate degree of privacy; clearly highly confidential conversations take place, which must not be overheard. In the design of courtrooms themselves, doors must be lobbied to maintain good sound insulation. For individual offices, doors will be acoustically rated.

As regards the overall design of courtroom spaces, there is some freedom in terms of shape, providing the reverberation time is controlled and the speech-reinforcement system can function well. An interesting example of an early twenty-first-century court building is Antwerp Law Courts by architects Rogers Stirk Harbour and Partners. The building contains eight main hearing rooms, each having a rectangular base, surmounted by a soaring roof structure composed of four geometric hyperbolic paraboloid forms. A hyperbolic paraboloid is a double curved surface, and the four sections are arranged with two upper ones and two lower ones forming a kind of 'oblique cone', which externally looks like a sail (Fig. 7.8a).

Fig. 7.8 Antwerp Law Courts: (a) external view, and (b) internal view. (Architects: Rogers Stirk Harbour. Photo: © Grant Smith/VIEW)

Fig. 7.8 *Continued.*

Internally, the surfaces of the hyperbolic paraboloids are criss-crossed by a timber lattice that is acoustically diffusing – there is no evidence of focusing by the curved surfaces in the occupied areas. Acoustic absorption is mainly located at low level where the participants are seated (Fig. 7.8b). The overall impression of these courtrooms is that they are light and airy, with the height providing a suitable degree of gravitas.

Transportation Buildings

Transportation buildings include airports, railway stations, underground train stations, bus stations and port terminals. In these buildings, the most important factor is that, under normal circumstances, passengers can clearly hear travel announcements so that they have the current information to know what to do. In an emergency, such as fire, both passengers and staff need immediate, highly intelligible spoken instructions to know how to evacuate the building. This information will not necessarily be the same in all parts of the building, as the evacuation may be zoned.

To achieve these high levels of speech intelligibility, the sound-reinforcement system must work very effectively. In objective terms, this means achieving a Speech Transmission Index (STI) of at least 0.5

(the range of STI is from 0 = bad to 1 = excellent). The value 0.5 is not particularly high and is classed as 'fair' speech intelligibility – but nevertheless it can be hard to achieve in large concourses of transportation buildings.

To achieve the required levels of STI, the speech-reinforcement system will need to be carefully designed, usually involving sophisticated column loudspeakers, but its success will depend on a controlled reverberation time. Controlling reverberation time to a suitably low level, which is usually taken as a mid-frequency value of 1.5 seconds, can be challenging in a large volume, and achievable values will depend on the amount of sound absorption that can be realistically installed.

In addition to controlling the reverberation time, it is also necessary to control ambient noise levels, as high levels degrade speech intelligibility. This can also be challenging, as transportation buildings inevitably involve noisy sources, such as aircraft taking off and trains pulling out of, or arriving in stations. With aircraft noise, it is possible to design the building envelope with high sound insulation, although controlling train noise on platforms is more difficult.

An example of acoustic treatment in a transportation building is Canary Wharf Station on the Jubilee extension of the London Underground; the station was designed by architects Foster and Partners. The concourse of the station is largely underground and is constructed as a concrete box, 300m (985ft) long and 30m (98ft) high, with a beautifully shaped concrete ceiling; *The Observer* newspaper likened the space to Canterbury Cathedral (*see* Fig. 7.9). At low level, the flank walls are lined with kiosks and administrative offices. Clearly the volume is very large indeed, and the criterion for the speech intelligibility of the public address system in this space was an STI of 0.5: a serious challenge.

To optimize the acoustic treatment to achieve an STI of 0.5, whilst at the same time maintaining the architectural aspirations of a basilica-like space with hard-wearing surface finishes such as fair-faced concrete, stainless steel and glass, an acoustic scale model was constructed at 1:50 scale (Fig. 7.10). The model was quite sophisticated in that not only could it reproduce the acoustic characteristics of the space at model scale, but it could also determine the Speech Transmission Index by using a model public address system.

A number of options was considered for acoustic treatment; the most suitable was to line the upper flank walls, the kiosk roofs and the ceiling with sound-absorbing material. Architecturally, lining the flank walls was acceptable, but applying acoustic material to the fair-faced concrete ceiling was not. To resolve this problem, a special design was

Fig. 7.9 Concourse of Canary Wharf Station, London. (Courtesy of Foster and Partners, Architects)

Fig. 7.10 1:50-scale acoustic model of Canary Wharf Station.

developed comprising stainless-steel tubes backed with sound-absorbing material. This maintained the aforementioned palette of hard-wearing materials, including stainless steel.

Open-Plan Offices

Open-plan offices are now the most common form of workplace for a wide range of office activities: they are considered to foster collaborative and innovative working. Also, they are cheaper to construct and easier to reconfigure than other types. However, poor acoustics can be detrimental to efficient office working, so it is important to optimize the acoustic design to make conditions acceptable.

The key requirements are to provide good communication at short distances, such as with fellow team members and also on the telephone, and to ensure acoustical privacy from other noise sources.

The overriding challenge is to achieve acoustical privacy, and in this respect larger offices, say with 100 occupants or more, tend to be more successful because they generate a steady background sound

that masks distracting noises. In smaller offices, the background sound tends to be sporadic and is therefore more intrusive.

Acoustic privacy can never be as good as in individual offices, but by implementing a range of acoustical measures, reasonable conditions can be achieved. These measures include separation of workstations by distance, sound absorptive treatments, screens and controlling levels of background sound.

Offices where the tasks are not prone to occasional distractions are less problematic than those where tasks require privacy and concentration. It is therefore important to separate by distance sensitive work areas from less sensitive ones. Also, noisy activities such as coffee/tea points, and noisy machinery such as photocopiers and printers should be distanced from work areas.

Fig. 7.11 shows the main sound paths between workstations, and possible attenuation methods. If these sound paths are not attenuated, then the sound will readily propagate throughout the office and reduce privacy. Attenuating these sound paths can be achieved by a combination of a sound-absorptive

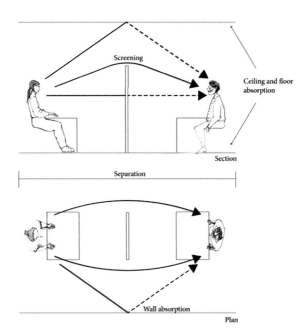

Fig. 7.11 Sound paths in an open-plan office.

commonly located in the ceiling. The background noise they produce can very effectively mask speech sounds and enhance privacy without being disturbing. The level of the masking sound should be very even throughout the office, within 3dBA, which can be achieved by having the loudspeakers laid out on a grid of between 2 to 4m (6 to 13ft). The sound the system produces should not be annoying; typically it is similar to ventilation system noise. A masking noise level of 45dBA is considered an appropriate value; it should not exceed 48dBA otherwise it will become disturbing in itself.

Implementing all the acoustic measures described above should provide enough privacy to make office working acceptable. However, in practice it has become evident that some activities require more privacy than an open-plan office can achieve, and this has led to the provision of various types of acoustic pods located within the office that can provide enhanced acoustic privacy.

There are countless variations on these types of pod, but a typical example is shown in Fig. 7.12. The pod effectively provides a tall screen around a number of occupants having a meeting, and all the surfaces of the pod are sound-absorbing. The screening and absorption reduce noise from the rest of the office, forming a haven where the meeting can take place without distraction. In addition, sounds from the meeting are attenuated and will not disturb other parts of the office.

ceiling and tall screens; a diffusing surface on the ceiling can also be beneficial. The ceiling absorption should be as powerful as possible, and care must be taken to ensure that the absorption does not decrease significantly at shallow angles of incidence that occur in long open-plan offices. Screens should be typically around 1.7m high and made from a material that has a sound reduction of 20dB or more – say, 18mm-thick plywood; they should also be sound absorbing on both sides.

Other acoustic treatments are beneficial but to a lesser extent. A carpet on the floor is helpful, and has the additional benefit of reducing footfall noise, and the sound of furniture scraping on a hard floor. Acoustic treatment on the walls is also helpful, although it is sometimes difficult to install if the walls are extensively glazed. Unfortunately, workstations adjacent to glazed walls can have less privacy because of wall reflections.

A further method of improving privacy is to use an electronic sound-masking system. Electronic sound-masking systems introduce a background noise into the office via loudspeakers, which are

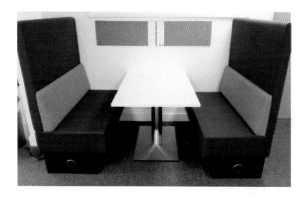

Fig. 7.12 Acoustic pod providing privacy in an open-plan office.

Fig. 7.13 Open-plan office at the European Headquarters for Bloomberg LP. (Courtesy Foster and Partners, Architects)

An outstanding example of a building containing innovative open-plan office configurations is the European headquarters for Bloomberg LP completed in 2017; it was designed by the architects Foster and Partners, with acoustic consultancy by Sandy Brown Associates (Fig. 7.13).

The ceiling is the most innovative part acoustically; it needed to be highly sound absorbing, and this degree of absorption was to be maintained even at shallow angles of incidence. To achieve this, the ceiling was designed as an open array of aluminium petals backed by acoustic absorption; the petal configuration also provides a degree of diffusion, which is of added benefit. Besides acoustics, the ceiling fulfils other roles, such as light reflectance and cooling.

The configuration of the desking was designed to encourage teamwork and collaboration. The desks are radial and laid out in clusters; this arrangement is good for team working and provides privacy from neighbours.

Museums

Museums and galleries should be pleasant spaces to be in from a sound point of view so that visitors can comfortably engage in viewing exhibits without undue distraction by others, or by ambient noise. Visitors should also be able to converse easily with accompanying friends, or clearly hear a guide during group tours.

Distraction by ambient noise can be annoying if the levels are too high, but it is relatively easy to control this noise. Ambient noise is likely to be a combination of the ingress of external noise and building services noise. The ingress of external noise is controlled by the sound insulation of the building envelope, which should be sufficient to ensure that internal residual levels are around 35dBA. Building services noise, which is usually dominated by ventilation noise, can be controlled with appropriate silencing, also to a level of around 35dBA.

One of the acoustical challenges in museums and galleries is that exhibition spaces are often interconnected so that noise can bleed from one space to another, causing disturbance. This challenge can be partly solved by separating the major spaces in the building by full-height partitions with doors. This still leaves interconnections between individual galleries – a partial solution is to adopt a strategic layout of tall screens coupled with acoustic absorption on ceiling and walls. A very successful solution was implemented at a museum in Vienna called Haus der Musik, which has numerous sonic displays. To avoid sound bleeding from one space to another, the display areas are joined by tunnel-like corridors whose walls, ceiling and floors are highly sound absorptive.

The overall ambience in museums and galleries should be one of quiet and calm, and in acoustical terms this means controlling the reverberation. A convenient method of controlling reverberation is to make the ceiling absorbent. Architecturally, this is often required to be a smooth white finish, and this can be achieved with an acoustic plaster type finish which is backed by a layer of mineral wool. An example of a sprayed acoustic plaster application at the Hayward Gallery in London is shown in Fig. 7.14.

At the Portland Collection Museum in Nottinghamshire, designed by Hugh Broughton

Fig. 7.14 Hayward Gallery, London: ceiling coffers finished with spray-applied acoustically porous plaster. (Courtesy Fielden Clegg Bradley Studio, Architects)

Fig. 7.15 Acoustic plaster on a barrel-vaulted ceiling. The Portland Collection, Welbeck Estate, by Hugh Broughton Architects. (Photo: © Hufton+Crow)

Architects with acoustics by Ramboll, the ceiling is barrel-vaulted, which introduced the problem of potential focusing; there was also the requirement for a calm atmosphere. Rendering the ceiling acoustically absorbent with a smooth plaster finish addressed both the reverberation and focusing issues (*see* Fig. 7.15).

If wall space is available for acoustic treatment, then this will also be beneficial. Wall treatment can take various forms, and at the Horniman Museum in London (*see* Fig. 7.16), it comprises perforated timber panels backed by mineral wool. The picture also shows acoustically absorbent panels, which help to separate the exhibits both visually and acoustically.

Fig. 7.16 Acoustic absorption and screens at the Horniman Museum, London.

Planetariums

Although planetariums are not built very frequently, they provide a very interesting exercise in acoustic and architectural design. The traditional form of a planetarium is a large dome surmounting a short cylinder in which the audience is located. Such domes cause a very strong focusing effect, where the focused reflection can be considerably stronger than the direct sound and can cause a disturbing echo. In his work on the Tonhalle in Düsseldorf, a former planetarium converted to a concert hall, Vercammen showed that the echo there exceeded the threshold for echo disturbance by around 14 decibels: a very substantial excess (Vercammen 2012). To mitigate the focusing, Vercammen referred to the three possible solutions proposed by the eminent German acoustician, Cremer (Cremer 1986).

Cremer stated that there are three methods for reducing focusing of sound, as shown in Fig. 7.17. The first method is to cover the concave surfaces with sound-absorptive material. A particular requirement of this solution is that the sound-absorptive material is thick so that the full range of frequencies is covered.

The second method is to make the concave curved surface diffusing by adding smaller scattering surfaces; this will result in the focused reflection becoming a diffuse reflection. The requirement here is that the depth of the scattering elements must be comparable to the wavelengths of sound, and so they need to be quite deep; a depth of 250mm (10in), for example,

would only cover mid frequencies but not low frequencies. Such projections can be considered either a challenge or an opportunity architecturally, and it must also be borne in mind that they will reduce the volume of the space to some extent.

The third method, which is particularly relevant to planetariums, is to avoid making the acoustic boundary focusing, but to make the visual boundary curved and acoustically transparent. This is possible by making the domed projection surface of finely perforated metal (for example, 25 per cent perforated aluminium sheet), which forms a screen for light waves but permits the passage of sound waves. The space behind the screen can be treated with sound-absorbing material to reduce reverberation.

A recent planetarium built in London is the Peter Harrison Planetarium situated in Greenwich Park, which is part of the National Maritime Museum; it was designed by Allies and Morrison architects and opened in 2007. The client was quite clear about the external form of the planetarium, in that it must not be a 'titty on the lawn', which meant not an external dome but some other relevant shape. This was an immediate advantage in terms of acoustical design as it avoided the construction of an external dome with its inherent focusing problems.

The form of the planetarium is a truncated cone with the north side tilted at 51.5 degrees to the horizontal, which is the latitude of Greenwich (*see* Fig. 7.18). The south side points at the local zenith, which is 90 degrees to the local horizon, and the top is slanted to be parallel to the celestial equator.

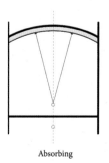

Absorbing

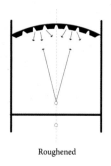

Roughened

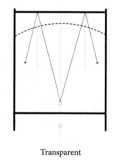

Transparent

Fig. 7.17 Methods of reducing focusing (after Cremer).

The cone was made of 225mm (9in) thick concrete to keep out external noise, particularly from aircraft, and the inside surface was sprayed with an acoustically absorbent cellulose fibre material to control the reverberation to low levels to provide suitable acoustic conditions for the sound-reinforcement system. The internal design of the planetarium comprised a perforated aluminium dome for projection, under which there are 120 seats, which recline to provide good sightlines. The low-level internal wall surrounding the seating is circular, but is fitted with timber battens to provide diffusion and to avoid focusing (*see* Fig. 7.19).

Fig. 7.18 External view of the Peter Harrison Planetarium at the Royal Observatory, Greenwich. (Architect: Allies and Morrison. Photo: Dennis Gilbert)

Summary

The buildings in this chapter have a variety of acoustical requirements, but what differentiates many of them from other buildings discussed in previous chapters is that they contain spaces where most people visit regularly, perhaps even daily – for example offices, railway stations, airports, worship spaces and so on. It is therefore very important that these spaces, which perhaps might be considered ordinary, are acoustically very successful. The outcome of acoustical success in these spaces is that the people can enjoy, amongst other things, calm working conditions, and can travel through pleasant public transport hubs that are safe.

Fig. 7.19 Inside view of the Peter Harrison Planetarium. (Architect: Allies and Morrison. Photo: Dennis Gilbert)

Future Possibilities

With the onset of the Corona virus in early 2020 and the subsequent lockdown, opera houses, concert halls, theatres, schools and offices were closed throughout the world.

A few smaller concert venues, such as the Wigmore Hall in London, managed to put on concerts of soloists or small ensembles without an audience which were broadcast, but this is proving more difficult for orchestras in larger halls. The influential conductors Sir Simon Rattle of the London Symphony Orchestra, and Mark Elder of the Hallé Orchestra, said that UK classical music could be devastated by the pandemic, with some orchestras possibly not surviving, and called on the government to provide support. They suggested that orchestral concerts are a live communion, a sharing of space, art and emotion, which is both vital and healing (*The Guardian*, 11 June 2020).

Concert halls and theatres will be among the last venues to resume normal operation, and at the time of writing there are no plans as to how and when this will happen, although trials are taking place of concerts with limited audiences. For these venues to fully open again, there may be new guidelines on how the musicians and the audience will have to socially distance – this will have an impact on both the music making and the allowable size of audiences; audience numbers clearly have an impact on ticket sales and income, and it may not be feasible for venues to operate.

The impact of these events on the future design of concert halls remains uncertain. If the return to a 'near normal' happens reasonably quickly, current concepts in concert hall design may prevail, and the argument between 'shoebox' and 'vineyard' types,

together with recent new typologies, may continue. On the other hand, a slow opening up of concert venues with guidelines on distancing between concert attendees may lead to new and innovative architectural concepts for concert hall design, although the acoustic parameters will not be able to change.

An example of an extreme architectural solution for maintaining social distancing was developed for the Victorian prison chapel at Lincoln Castle, as shown in Fig. 8.1, where screens were placed between inmates so that they could not see each other but each could see and hear the central preacher – the social distancing in that case was not, of course, for health reasons. Although this is an extreme example, it demonstrates that effective architectural solutions are possible.

A more recent concept has been proposed by Pierre Chican for cinemas where the audience is seated in individual balconies, not unlike the boxes in early opera houses. The balconies would enable social distancing, but for a different reason from the original Baroque venues.

For schools, to maintain the wellbeing of the children it was, of course, necessary for them to return as soon as possible. In the standard classroom situation there is little change in acoustical terms, except that the students will be more separated from each other, and probably fewer per class, which will reduce background levels slightly. However, the open-plan classroom, with all its inherent acoustic problems of distraction by noise and poor speech intelligibility, may no longer be feasible, because mixing between different class groups may not be allowed. This would be beneficial acoustically in the overall teaching arrangements in schools. In the case of

Fig. 8.1
Segregation of
inmates in
a Victorian
prison chapel at
Lincoln Castle.

Fig. 8.2 A possible design for social distancing in future auditoria
(from a concept by Pierre Chican).

music teaching, individual lessons and playing in small ensembles will be possible, but orchestras will be subject to the same difficulties as their professional counterparts.

In the case of offices, it was surprising during lockdown how effective home working became, with many people reporting that their productivity had increased during the first two months. The journalist Kerstin Sailer has claimed that this is an opportunity to reimagine the office (Sailer 2020). With the easing of lockdown and the development of a vaccine, it is important to consider how the future office should be designed. There have been many experiments with open-plan office working, with such concepts as the 'action office' and 'activity-based working', but none have been totally successful. Occupants have been distracted by excessive noise, while being often denied the community-building aspects of casual encounters and conversations. The more recent 'hot-desking' arrangements, where office workers share desks, which is effectively a cost-saving exercise, does not benefit users from constantly chopping and changing their work environment.

Prior to the onset of the Corona virus, the large corporations had lauded the highly innovative office with facilities such as table tennis, slides and bean bags. The same corporations are now saying that this is not necessary, and that working from home is good. However, research suggests that face-to-face interactions are important drivers of new ideas, an effect known as 'strength of weak ties', and this has been lacking in home working. Therefore it is important in the office of the future that facilities are provided for sharing experiences: this is necessary for the social interactions and exchange of ideas that ultimately lead to the success of the organization. This will require well designed spaces with good acoustics where people can converse in a calm environment, share ideas, and work towards a common goal.

Glossary of Acoustical Terms

Absorption coefficient, α A measure of the proportion of sound energy incident on a surface that is absorbed. Values of absorption coefficient range from 0 to 1; a surface that has absorbed no sound has an absorption coefficient of 0, and a surface that absorbs all sound incident on it has an absorption coefficient of 1.

A-weighting The human ear is less sensitive to low and very high frequencies than it is to those in the range 500Hz to 4kHz. This frequency response can be represented by an A-weighting filter. The A-weighting correction can be applied to a sound spectrum to give a better correlation to a subjective response. An A-weighted level is denoted by an 'A' subscript in the descriptor L_{Aeq} or an 'A' in brackets following the decibel unit, ie dB(A).

Clarity Index, C_{80} Clarity Index is an objective measure of the balance between the clarity and reverberance of music within a space. It is evaluated by taking the ratio of the early sound to the late sound in an impulse response; this ratio is then expressed in decibels by taking the logarithm and multiplying it by 10. Early sound is that sound which arrives within 80ms of the direct sound and the late sound is that sound which arrives after 80ms.

Decibel The unit used to define sound pressure level relative to a reference pressure, which approximates to the threshold of human hearing. The ratio of the measured sound pressure to the reference is expressed in decibels by taking the logarithm and multiplying it by 20.

Direct sound The sound that travels directly from a sound source (vocal or musical instrument) to the listener's ear. It is the first sound to reach the listener having travelled by the shortest path at a velocity of approximately 340ms⁻¹. The direct sound is normally the key component affecting the intelligibility of speech and the clarity of music.

Early decay time (EDT) Evaluates the time taken for the first 10dB of the reverberant decay as opposed to the full 60dB decay, which is defined for reverberation time. The EDT value is then multiplied by 6 so that a direct comparison can be made with reverberation time. EDT is considered to be more significant in the perception of reverberation and can vary with different locations in an auditorium, whereas reverberation time stays more or less constant.

Early energy fraction A metric correlated with the intelligibility of speech. It is the fraction of the total energy in an impulse response arriving within 50ms of the direct sound.

Early lateral energy fraction A measure of the subjective effect of the broadening of a sound source such as an orchestra in a concert hall. It is considered to be a very desirable effect when listening to music and is created by reflections arriving at the listener from the sides; ie lateral reflections. It is measured by the ratio between the early energy (5 to 80ms) received by a figure-of-eight microphone with its null pointing at the source and the early energy (0–80ms) received by an omnidirectional microphone at the same position.

Early reflections Shortly after the direct sound arrives, the listener in an auditorium or other space receives a series of sound reflections which have been reflected one or more times from room boundaries such as walls and ceiling. Reflections which arrive within approximately 50ms contribute to speech intelligibility. Those which arrive within approximately 80ms contribute to clarity in music.

Equivalent continuous sound level, $L_{Aeq,T}$ The equivalent continuous sound pressure level is an energy average and is defined as the level of a notional sound: over a defined period of time, that would deliver the same A-weighted sound energy as a fluctuating sound.

Frequency The rate of repetition of a sound wave. The subjective equivalent in music is pitch. The unit of frequency is hertz (Hz) which is identical to cycles per second.

Impact sound insulation Impacts on a building structure such as footsteps on a floor cause the structure to vibrate, and this vibration radiates sound into other rooms in the building. Impact sound can be reduced by using materials that reduce the energy of an impact; carpet on floors is a simple example.

Impulse response The response of a room to an impulsive sound with the sound source and receiver located at specific locations. The impulse response will vary to some extent with location. It normally comprises the direct sound at the beginning of the response, which is followed by a sequence of reflections that gradually decay with time.

Level difference, D The sound level difference between two spaces with a sound source in one of them.

Mid-frequency reverberation time, T_{mf} The average value of the reverberation times in the three octave bands, 500Hz, 1kHz and 2kHz. T_{mf} is a key metric in Building Bulletin 93, 'Acoustic Design of Schools'.

Octave band An octave is a frequency interval between two sounds whose frequency ratio is 2 (eg from 707Hz to 1,414Hz), and an octave band is the range of frequencies contained in an octave (all frequencies from 707Hz to 1,414Hz). Octave bands are described by their centre frequency (the 707Hz–1,414Hz band is called the 1kHz octave band).

Reverberation time, T In general terms, the reverberation time is the time taken in seconds for a loud sound within a space to decay to inaudibility after the sound source has stopped. More specifically, it is the time taken for the sound to decay by 60 decibels. Reverberation time is an important indicator of the acoustic quality of a space.

Sound reduction index, R Sound reduction index is a measure of the ability of a building component to resist the transmission of sound. It is a property of the building construction only, independent of its area and the reverberation time in the receiving room. It is obtained in a laboratory test.

Speech Transmission Index (STI) A measure of speech transmission quality. It is a metric whose values vary between 0 = bad to 1 = excellent. On this scale, an STI of 0.5 provides acceptable speech intelligibility.

Standardized level difference, D_{nT} The sound level difference between a pair of rooms standardized to a reference reverberation time.

Strength, G Strength, which is expressed in dB, is related to the judgement of loudness in auditoria. It can be measured by placing a calibrated omnidirectional sound source, usually on the stage, and recording an impulse response at a given location. Strength is then evaluated as the logarithmic ratio of the sound energy of the measured impulse response to that of the response measured in the free field at a distance of 10m from the sound source. Values for strength in concert halls normally fall in the range 0 to +10dB.

Wavelength The distance between successive crests of a wave.

Weighted sound reduction index and weighted level difference, R_w and D_w The sound reduction indices and the level differences over the frequency range of 100Hz to 3,150Hz (in third octaves) can be weighted in accordance with a standard weighting curve to give a single figure descriptor.

I am particularly grateful to Megan Makinson, a final year student at the Bartlett School of Architecture, for preparing all the diagrams and drawings, and to my wife, Liz, for helping to compile the contents.

Many thanks also to the numerous architects and acousticians with whom I have collaborated, and who have kindly provided me with images of their projects to illustrate the text.

Finally I would like to express gratitude to all the people I have had the pleasure of working with in my career in both teaching and practice, who have encouraged me along my acoustics path, especially colleagues at university and at Arup and Ramboll. It has been a particular privilege to have been mentored by a number of inspirational acousticians, notably Peter Parkin, Michael Barron and Derek Sugden.

CHAPTER 1. FUNDAMENTALS OF ACOUSTICS

Vitruvius (translated by Morgan, M.H.) (1960) *The ten books on architecture*, New York: Dover Publications.

Yost, William A. (2000) *Fundamentals of Hearing: an introduction* (4th ed.), Academic Press.

Sabine, Wallace Clement (1922) Collected papers on acoustics, Harvard University Press.

Marshall, A.H. and Barron, M. (2001) 'Spatial responsiveness in concert halls and the origins of spatial impression', in *Applied Acoustics* 62, pp. 91–108.

CHAPTER 2. OPERA HOUSES AND CONCERT HALLS (PRE-TWENTIETH CENTURY)

Bonsi, Davide. (2012) 'The acoustic analysis of Palladio's Teatro Olimpico, Vicenza' in *The Music Room in Early Modern France and Italy*, pp. 277–289 (Eds Deborah Howard and Laura Moretti), Oxford University Press.

D'Orazio, D. and Nannini, S. 'Towards Italian opera houses: a review of acoustic design in pre-Sabine scholars' in *Acoustics* 2019, *1*, pp. 252–280.

Forsyth, Michael (1985) *Buildings for Music*, Cambridge University Press.

Barron, Michael (2010) *Auditorium Acoustics and Architectural Design*, Spon Press.

Newton, J. P. (2001) 'Room acoustics measurements at the Royal Opera House, London' Proceedings of the 17th International Congress on Acoustics, Rome, Vol lll, pp. 34–35.

Vercammen, M., Lautenbach, M. and Metkemeijer, R. (2019) 'Concertgebouw Amsterdam: history of the main hall and its acoustics; part 2: preserving the acoustics' Proceedings of the International Symposium on room acoustics. Amsterdam.

CHAPTER 3. OPERA HOUSES AND CONCERT HALLS (TWENTIETH TO TWENTY-FIRST CENTURIES)

Loos, Adolf (1912) 'Das Mysterium der Akustik' in *Der Merker. Osterreichische Zeitschrift fur Musik und Theater*, vol. 3, issue1/1, pp. 9f.

Sabine, Wallace Clement (1922) Collected papers on acoustics, Harvard University Press.

Beranek, L.L. (2004) *Concert Halls and Opera Houses. Music acoustics and architecture* (2nd ed.) Springer, New York.

Forsyth, Michael (1985) *Buildings for Music*, Cambridge University Press.

Marshall, A.H. and Barron, M. (2001) 'Spatial responsiveness in concert halls and the origins of spatial impression' in *Applied Acoustics*, 62, pp. 91–108.

Parkin, P.H. and Morgan, K. (1965) '"Assisted Resonance" in the Royal Festival Hall, London' in *Journal of Sound and Vibration*, 2, pp. 74–85.

Jordan, V.L. (1973) 'Acoustical design considerations of the Sydney Opera House' in *Journal and Proceedings of the Royal Society of New South Wales*, Vol. 106, Parts 1 and 2.

Marshall, A.H. (1967) 'A note on the importance of room cross-section in concert halls' in *Journal of Sound and Vibration*, 5, pp. 100–112.

Barron, Michael (1971) 'The subjective effects of first reflections in concert halls – the need for lateral reflections' in *Journal of Sound and Vibration*, 15, pp. 475–494.

Schroeder, M.R. (1975) 'Diffuse sound reflection by maximum-length sequences' in *Journal of the Acoustical Society of America*, 57(1), pp. 149–150.

Barron, Michael (2010) *Auditorium Acoustics and Architectural Design*, Spon Press.

Beranek, L.L. (2016) 'Concert hall acoustics: recent findings' in *Journal of the Acoustical Society of America*, 139, p. 1,548.

Marshall, A.H. and Day, C. (2015) 'The conceptual acoustical design for La Philharmonie de Paris, Grand Salle. Proceedings of the 9th International conference on Auditorium Acoustics in Paris held by the Institute of Acoustics.

Scelo, T., Valentine, J., Marshall, H. and Day, C. (2015) 'Implementing the acoustical concept for La Philharmonie de Paris, Grand Salle'. Proceedings of the 9th International conference on Auditorium Acoustics in Paris held by the Institute of Acoustics.

Oguchi, K., Quiquerez, M. and Toyota, Y. (2018) 'Acoustical design of Elbphilharminie'. Proceedings of the 10th International conference on Auditorium Acoustics in Hamburg held by the Institute of Acoustics.

Kesting, J. Frankfurter Allgemeine, 08.02.2019. https://www.faz.net/-gfs-9jlx3

CHAPTER 4. THE ACOUSTICS OF THEATRES

Knudsen, V.O. (1932) *Architectural Acoustics*, John Wiley, New York, pp. 497–500.

Barron, Michael (2010) *Auditorium Acoustics and Architectural Design*, Spon Press.

Mackintosh, Iain (2011) *The Guthrie Thrust Stage: A Living Legacy*. Published by the Association of British Theatre Technicians on the occasion of the 2011 Prague Quadrennial of Scenography and Theatre Architecture.

CHAPTER 5. THE ACOUSTICS OF SCHOOLS

Bagenal, H. and Wood, A. (1931) *Planning for Good Acoustics*, Methuen, London.

Keath, M.P.K. (1983) *The Development of School Construction Systems*, 1946–64. PhD, Thames Polytechnic, London.

The Acoustics Committee of the Building Research Board of Scientific & Industrial Research (1944) 'Sound Insulation and Acoustics', HMSO, London.

Parkin, P.H. and Humphries, H.R. (1963) *Acoustics, Noise and Buildings*, Faber and Faber, London.

Building Bulletin 30 (1966) 'Secondary school design: drama and music', Department of Education and Science, HMSO, London.

Building Bulletin 51 (1975) 'Acoustics in educational buildings', Department for Education and Employment, HMSO, London.

Design of educational facilities for deaf children (1980) British Journal of Audiology, Supplement No. 3, pp. 1–8.

Building Bulletin 87 (Revision of Design Note 17) (1997) 'Guidelines for environmental design in schools', Department for Education and Employment, HMSO.

Building Bulletin 93 (2003) 'Acoustics design of schools. A design Guide', Department for Education and Skills. The Stationery Office.

Building Bulletin 93 (2015) 'Acoustics design of schools: performance standards', Department for Education.

Acoustics of schools: a design guide (2015) Published jointly by the Institute of Acoustics and the Association of Noise Consultants.

CHAPTER 6. MUSIC SCHOOLS AND RECITAL HALLS

Building Bulletin 30 (1966) 'Secondary school design: drama and music', Department of Education and Science, HMSO, London.

Building Bulletin 51 (1975) 'Acoustics in educational buildings', Department for Education and Employment, HMSO, London.

Building Bulletin 86 (1997). Updated version published in 2010 'Music accommodation in secondary schools – a design guide', Department for Education and Employment, HMSO.

Building Bulletin 93 (2015) 'Acoustics design of schools: performance standards', Department for Education.

Cox, T.J. and D'Antonio, P. (2004) *Acoustic Absorbers and Diffusers*, Spon Press, London, p. 54.

The Architectural Review (May 2002) 'Harmonic scale', pp. 70–74.

Wulfrank, Thomas (2006) 'Acoustic analysis of Wigmore Hall, London, in the context of the 2004 refurbishment'. Proceedings of the International conference on Auditorium Acoustics in Copenhagen held by the Institute of Acoustics, Vol: 28 Pt 2.

CHAPTER 7. OTHER BUILDING TYPES

Cox, Trevor (August 2010) 'Acoustic archaeology: the secret sounds of Stonehenge' in *New Scientist*.

Howard, D. and Moretti, (2009) *Sound and Space in Renaissance Venice*, Yale University Press, New Haven and London.

Vercammen, M. (2012) 'Sound concentration caused by curved surfaces', PhD thesis, Eindhoven University of Technology. Published as issue 163 in the *Bouwstenen* series.

Cremer, L. and Muller, H.A. (translated by Schultz, T.J.) (1982) *Principles and Applications of Room Acoustics*, Volume 1, Applied Science Publishers, London and New York.

Abramovitz, M. 53
acoustic absorption 21
acoustic drapes 117
Acoustics of schools: a design guide 105
Aldeburgh Festival 121
Aleotti, G.B. 30
Algarotti, F. 32
Allies and Morrison (architects) 52, 250
Apfel, R.E. 6
Antwerp Law Courts 143
Artec Consultants (acoustics) 65, 67
Arup (acoustics) 37, 67, 69, 73, 122–126,
    129, 131
Ashton, Raggatt, McDougall (architects) 73
Atelier Jean Nouvel (architect) 77
Avery Fisher Hall 55

Bagnall, H. 49
Bagnall and Wood 96
Barbican Concert Hall 60
Barron, M 27, 32, 39, 44, 50, 59, 66, 67, 81, 83, 91
Barry, E.M. 36
Basilica di San Marco 138
Bell, A.G. 12
bel 12
Benslow Music 132
Beranek, L. 47, 48, 53, 67
Berlin Philharmonie 56
Birmingham Symphony Hall 65
Blonski and Heard (architects) 91, 93
Bloomberg European HQ 148
Bonsi, D 30
Boston Symphony Hall 44, 46
Bridge Theatre, London 94
Bridgewater Hall 67
Britten, B. 121
Britten Studio 125
Bruckwald, O. 38
Building Bulletins
    30, secondary school design, drama and music
        98, 110
    51, acoustics in educational buildings 98, 110
    86, music accommodation in secondary schools
        99, 110
    87, guidelines for environmental design in
        schools 98

93, acoustic design of schools, a design guide 99, 110,
    111
Building Regulations 99
Building Research Station 49, 50
Burrell, Foley, Fischer (architects) 127

Cambridge University 90
Cambridge Mosque 142
Canary Wharf Station 145
Carnegie Hall 53
Chetham's School of Music 132
Chican, P. 153
Chichester Festival Theatre 91, 94
Christchurch Town Hall 59
Clarendon Muse 130
clarity index 27
Collcutt, T. 135
column loudspeaker 140
compression 9
Concertgebouw, Amsterdam 39, 43
Cosmo Rodewald Concert Hall 131
Covent Garden 36
Cox, T. 134, 138
Cremer, L. 56, 58, 150
cross-laminated timber 127
Crossways Church 142
Crucible Theatre, Sheffield 94
Cuvilliés, F. 33
Cuvilliés Theatre 33

decibel 11
Den Norske Opera, Oslo 68
Design of educational facilities for deaf children 98
Design Note 17 98
diffraction 10
diffusion 115
direct sound 16
Dixon Jones (architects) 37

ear 12
early decay time 22
early energy fraction 26, 82
early reflections 16–28
Eastman Theatre, Rochester 48
Education Act (1944) 97
Education (school premises) Regulations (1966) 98

Edward Boyle Auditorium 122
Edwina Palmer Hall 132
Eisenstadt 39
Elbphilharmonie 79
Elisabeth Murdoch Hall 73
Epidauros 6, 16, 17, 29, 81, 89
Esterházy 39
equal-loudness curves 13

Festspielhaus, Bayreuth 37
Fisher, A. 55
floating floor 112
flutter echo 114
Fogg Art Museum 20, 30
Forsyth, M. 30, 31, 32, 48
Foster and Partners (architects) 145, 148
Fowkes, F 40
frequency 9

Galli Bibiena 32
Garnier, C. 37
Geffen, D. 53, 55
Globe Theatre 84
Glyndebourne Opera House 68, 93
Glyndebourne Touring Opera 93
Grand Theatre, Bordeaux 35
Grange Park Opera House 71
Gropius, W. 96
Guangzhou Opera House 68, 72
Guthrie, W. 94

Haas effect 140
Hackney Empire Theatre 88
Hadid, Z. 72
Hall, P. 58
Harris, C. 55
Haworth Tompkins (architects) 125
Haydn, J. 39
Haydnsaal 39
Hayward Gallery 148
Helmholz resonators 24
hertz 10
Herzhog & de Meuron (architects) 79
Hoffmann Building 126
Hopkins Architects 69
Horniman Museum 149
Howard, D. 137
Hugh Broughton Architects 138
Hyde, J. 62, 63

Impington Village College 96
impulse response 16, 18, 26
initial time delay gap 53
Ingarden and Ewy (architects) 75
Izosaki, A. 75
Jacqueline du Pré 122

Jerwood Kiln Studio 126
Jordan, V. 58
Johnson, R. 55, 65
Juillard School of Music 53

Kahle Acoustics 77
Kaufman, J. 80
Keath, M. 96
Knudsen, V. 81
Konserthus, Gothenberg 49
Koussevitzky Music Shed 53
Krakow Concert Hall 75

Lasdun, D. 89
lateral efficiency 27
Lawrence, C. 62
le Corbusier 6
Lincoln Center for the Performing Arts 53
Loos, A. 6, 46
Lucerne 66, 77
Lyon, G. 48

Mackintosh, I. 94
Markgrafliches Opernhaus 32
Marks Barfield (architects) 142
Marshall, A.H. 27, 50, 59, 62, 73, 77
Marshall Day (acoustics) 60, 62, 72, 77
Martin, L. 49
Martin Harris Centre 130
Matcham, F. 88
Matthew, R. 49
Mengelberg, W. 44
Merritt Centre 127
Metropolitan Opera Association 53
Milton Keynes Theatre 91
Moretti, L. 137
Morgan, M. 8
Musikvereinssaal 39

Nagata Acoustics 77, 79
Nannini 30, 32
Neues Gewandhaus, Leipzig 43, 46
New York Philharmonic Hall 53
New York Times 54
Newton, J. 37
Niccolini 6
normal modes 10

octave bands 15
Oguchi 79
Old Boston Music Hall 46
Olivier, L. 89, 91
Olivier Theatre 89
Operaen, Copenhagen 68
Orazio 30, 32
Palladio, A. 6, 30, 83, 137, 138

Pamoja Concert Hall 123
panel absorption 24
Paoletti, D. 62
Paris Opera 37
Paris Philharmonie 77
Parkin, P. 50, 97
pascals 11
Patel Taylor (architects) 132
Penderecki, K. 75
Percy Thomas Partnership (architects) 65
Peter Harrison Planetarium 150
Peutz (acoustics) 45
phons 12
porous absorbers 22
Portland Collection 149
Pythagoras 6

Quiquerez 79

Ramboll 71, 75, 127, 142, 149
rarefaction 9
Redentore 138
Residenz Theatre 33
reverberation 19
reverberation chamber 65
reverberation time 7, 19–22, 113
RHWL (architects) 67
Rogers Stirk Harbour (architects) 143
Roger Stephenson (architects) 132
Royal Albert Hall 40
Royal Festival Hall 49
Royal Shakespeare Theatre 94

Sabine, W.C. 7, 20, 29, 46, 47
Sailer, K. 153
Salle Pleyel 48
Sandy Brown Associates (acoustics) 148
San Francesco della Vigna 138
San Giorgio Maggiore 138
Sansovino, J. 137
Scharoun, H. 56
Schonberg, H. 54
Schroeder, M. 63, 76
Segerstrom Hall 62
Semper, G. 37
Sevenoaks School 123
Severance Hall 48
Shakespeare Festival Theatre, Ontario 94
Shakespeare, W. 84
Sherborne Girls School 127
Shield, B. 99
Snape Maltings 121
sound absorption 22
sound absorption coefficient 22

sound attenuator 111
sound pressure 9
speech transmission index 104, 109, 144
standing wave 10, 117
St David's Hall 75
Stoller Concert Hall 131
strength 27
Sugden, D. 121
Sydney Opera House 58
Szeliski, J. 62

Tanglewood Music Shed 53
Teatro alla Scala 33, 34, 71
Teatro Farnese 30
Teatro Olimpico 6, 30, 83
Teatro Regio 32
Teatro San Carlo 6, 33
Teatro San Cassiano 31
Teatro SS Giovanni e Paolo 31
Theatre Projects (consultants) 69
Theatre Royal, Bury St Edmunds 86
Theatre Royal Drury Lane 35, 85
Theatre Royal, Plymouth 91
thrust stage 91, 94
Tim Ronalds Architects 71, 89, 123, 129
Tonhalle, Dusseldorf 43, 150
Toyota, Y. 77, 79

Utzon, J. 58

van Gendt, D. 43
van Heyningen and Haward (architects) 122
Vercammen, M. 45, 150
Vitruvius 6, 8, 137
vHH (architects) 142

Wagner, R. 37
Warren and Mahoney (architects) 59
Waterfront Hall 75
Watford Grammar School 129
Watson, F. 48
wavelength 9
Weber-Fechner Law 11
Welsh National Opera 93
Wigmore Hall 134
Willaert, A. 137
Wilton's Music Hall 87
Wren, C. 85
Wulfrank, T. 135

Yost 11
Young Vic Theatre 94

Zorzi, F. 137, 138